SUCCESSFUL INDUCTION

SUCCESSFUL INDUCTION

How to get the most from your new employees

JUDY SKEATS

First published in 1991

Kogan Page Limited
120 Pentonville Road
London N1 9JN

British Library Cataloguing in Publication Data

A CIP record for this book is available from the British Library.

ISBN 0-7494-0465-5

Typeset by Saxon Printing Ltd, Derby
Printed and bound in Great Britain by
Clays, St Ives plc

Contents

Introduction 9

1. **The Importance of Induction** **11**
The stress of a new job *11*
The 'induction crisis' and costs of early leaving *12*
What is induction? *16*
Is induction worth the cost and effort? *18*

2. **The Behavioural Contract** **20**
Company literature *22*
The impact of the interview *23*
The supervisor's influence *23*
Peer pressure *24*
Influencing the psychological contract *25*

3. **Pre-employment Preparation** **28**
Pre-employment information *28*
Behind the scenes *32*
The induction policy *35*
3.1 Pre-induction checklist *38*
3.2 Letter offering a job *39*
3.3 Letter containing joining instructions *42*
3.4 Welcome letter *44*
3.5 Checklist of Welcome Pack enclosures *45*
3.6 Notification of engagement sheet – for personnel use *46*

4. **The First Few Days** **48**
Immediate needs *49*
In the first weeks *57*
4.1 Induction notes for supervisors *59*
4.2 Supervisor's induction checklist *61*
4.3 Sample timetable for office worker's first and second days *64*
4.4 Checklists for induction topics *66*

5. Elements of a Successful Induction Course **72**
Designing the induction programme *72*
Learning styles and training methods *77*
Skill acquisition and job training *84*
Induction manuals and employees' log books *88*
5.1 Trainer/administrator's checklist for an induction course *89*
5.2 Letter inviting newcomers to the induction course *92*
5.3 Induction course details and programme *93*
5.4 Traditional induction course timetable *94*

6. Catering for Particular Needs **98**
People with disabilities *98*
Part-timers and shift-workers *99*
Distant workers and professionals *100*
Women returners *101*
Ethnic minorities *102*
School leavers *102*
New graduates and college leavers *104*
Managers and executives *106*
Expatriates *108*
Transferees, promotees and members of project teams *110*
After the organisation's redundancies *111*
After the individual's unemployment *112*
Older workers *112*
Temporary staff *112*
Points for particular industrial groups *113*

7. Longer-term Needs **115**
Settling in *115*
Giving feedback *116*
Further information needs *121*
Probationary period and potential problems *122*
Career planning *125*
7.1 End of probation review form and notes for guidance *127*
7.2 Letter confirming employment *131*
7.3 Letter extending the probationary period *132*
7.4 Dismissal letter *133*
7.5 Appraisal record form and notes for guidance *134*
7.6 Notes for guidance for those undergoing appraisal *139*

8. Evaluation of Induction **142**
Who should be involved? *142*
Time-scales for evaluation *143*
Quantitative measures *143*
Qualitative measures *145*

Effective evaluation *148*
8.1 Induction course evaluation form *150*
8.2 Induction log book *153*
8.3 Questions for use in structured exit interviews *154*

9. Further Reading and Information **155**

Index **158**

A note about the use of language

I want to explain my use of singular verbs with the apparently plural pronouns 'they', 'them' or 'their'. This approach was successfully used by Richard Nelson Bolles is his classic book on job search, *What Color is Your Parachute*? He asserts that the pronoun 'they' was once treated as both plural and singular in the English language, just as 'you' is. However, the usage changed at a time in English history when agreement in number was more important than agreement in gender. Faced today with such artifices as he/she or s/he, the time may now have come to bring back the earlier usage of 'they'. Given the sexist consciousness of most audiences these days, agreement in gender has once again become more important than agreement in number. This usage is quite common in spoken English and on many signs, eg 'Anyone using this car park does so at their own risk', etc. I have therefore adopted this approach as a useful way round the he/she problem. It also seemed apt, as this book is designed for those who will be organising the induction of staff, one or many.

I also wish to clarify my use of '(line) manager', 'boss' and 'supervisor' in the text. I have used these words interchangeably, to indicate the immediate superior of the person being inducted. Where I have addressed the reader as 'you' I have assumed that they are this person.

Introduction

Induction is a much neglected area of management. It is more than a matter of simple courtesy and greeting the new employees properly. It involves not just job training for new staff, but the whole process of integrating them into the organisation and 'orientation', as the North Americans say.

How often have you heard new employees saying despairingly 'I didn't know it was supposed to be done like that!'? Perhaps you've heard of managers who left a new recruit at a desk on their own all day and then seemed surprised when they didn't come back? These kinds of problem are symptomatic of poor induction, of not having taken sufficient care of these valuable new assets.

The pool of potential employees is increasingly diverse in terms of age, language and cultural background, etc. There is therefore more need than ever to pay proper attention to induction, which may not happen naturally owing to cultural and psychological barriers. Management must decide how long *they* want employees to stay, rather than adopting a *laissez-faire* style, leaving it all to chance. This question may be key to the development plans for the business. New employees are the building blocks through whom the organisation can lay the foundations for the future.

Employers will almost certainly pay care and attention to detail when deciding how, where and when new equipment should be installed, and who should look after it and maintain it. Yet surprisingly few pay more than lip service to ensuring that new employees are sufficiently integrated to play an active role in the company as early as possible. It is self-evident that new employees cannot be effective instantly. It takes time to adjust and get to know the job.

The aim of induction is to integrate new or promoted employees so that they become effective as quickly as possible. Research has shown that the influence of the first few days has a lasting effect on performance and on staff turnover, and that the rewards in terms of goodwill, morale and work efficiency greatly outweigh the effort and investment required to make the new employee feel at home. Additionally, early leaving is reduced by effective initial training, particularly if the selection process has been similarly intensive. It therefore follows that good induction makes sound business sense.

What can this book do for you?

This book is primarily designed for personnel managers, line managers and students – in fact, anyone concerned with induction. It is a practical handbook which attempts to give you all you need to design and run effective inductions and undertake the necessary follow-up, whether you work in a large or a small company, and whether you intend to run a formal induction course or not. It also gives the reasons why the recommendations are made. Your own programme can be tailored from the information given – take what is useful and omit what is not applicable in your organisation.

The text covers not only direct methods to bring the performance of newcomers up to standard quickly, but concentrates on how to make them feel better and integrate faster. This is not to say that you have recruited weaklings who need protection, but that there is strong evidence to suggest that this will indirectly help all new employees to perform better. It will help your company image too.

The book begins by showing you the importance of induction, why it is carried out and the benefits it can yield. This will help you to convince your employer of the value of the induction and the reasons why you should be given a budget for it! Chapter 2 covers the 'behavioural contract', that is, the factors influencing motivation and elements that an individual takes into account, consciously or not, when deciding how to act in a new job. Chapter 3 looks at the pre-induction phase, the preparation stage before the new recruit arrives on the company doorstep. It includes some very basic elements which none the less are often forgotten in the rush to get everything ready.

Chapter 4 covers the first days and weeks in the new job, with practical guidance and dos and don'ts for managers and employers. Chapter 5 looks at the factors to be taken into account when designing an induction course, and the importance of learning styles and theory on the programme constructed for newcomers. Chapter 6 covers special needs for certain groups of employees and Chapter 7 shows what steps should be taken following on from the individual's first weeks and how to maintain and improve their level of performance. Chapter 8 covers evaluation of the induction programme, an oft-forgotten but very important area. As with all training, the induction programme can only continue to be useful and cost-effective if properly monitored, so that any changes in the organisation or the needs of the new employees are taken into account and the programme amended accordingly.

Throughout the book are checklists, memory prompters and examples of standard letters in order to make it of immediate practical use to the busy manager.

Chapter 1

The Importance of Induction

The stress of a new job

Starting a new job is considered by psychologists to be one of the most stressful life experiences for most people. Other major stressors include moving house, so if your new employee has moved areas to join your company, the effects of stress may be even more marked.

The more you can help the individual to settle in and reduce their anxieties, the better they will be able to concentrate on the job and learn about the organisation. If they are unable to settle, they are unlikely to respond quickly and effectively to the demands of the job and the time taken for them to reach full productivity will be delayed.

One of the prime aims of induction or job orientation is the removal of the 'unknowns'. New employees will need to acclimatise to the people, the surroundings, the job, the company and perhaps the industry if they do not already know it. As well as excitement, they will have lots of worries and anxieties about the new position and about possible mistakes or *faux pas* they might make on the first day. The most important are:

Will I be able to do my new job?
Will I fit in?
Will I make a good impression on the boss?

Others include the who, what, where, how, when and why:

Who will be my friends and colleagues?
do I report to?
will answer my questions?
will judge my work?

What am I expected to do?
are the projects, tasks or deadlines I am responsible for?
is a typical day like?

Where is my desk and work area?
are the people and departments I will need to make contact with?
are the things I need – the coffee room, the toilets, the parking, the photocopier, the tools, etc?

How will I learn about the job?
do I fill in the forms?
do I order supplies or get equipment mended?
do I answer the telephone or use the computer, etc?

When should I arrive and leave work?
are the peaks and troughs in the workload (if any)?
is overtime required?
will I be paid?
are holidays taken?
will my probationary period finish?

Why must I follow that procedure?
does the company adopt this policy?
do I have to do this task when other colleagues do not?

Individuals should not be expected just to 'pick it up as they go along'. If you adopt a philosophy of 'sink or swim' management by throwing your new recruits in at the deep end, you must be prepared to fish out the floating corpses of the non-swimmers. Naturally there is a balance to be maintained between this and bombarding them with reams of excess information; induction needs to be properly structured and paced.

The new recruit will need to make a number of adjustments to get used to the new environment, and 'the way we do things around here'. This can be no less true for promotees, particularly if their promotion involves a change of department where the culture can be quite different.

The 'induction crisis' and costs of early leaving

Many new employees leave after just a few weeks, before they have had a chance to make a real contribution. Voluntary resignation has been called a 'haemorrhage of talent and investment'.

This is expensive for the company and less than useful for the individual. Organisations spend thousands of pounds on recruitment and training – all wasted if the new recruit does not stay. However, this is not an uncommon occurrence. The 'induction crisis' is well documented. It is a persistent and marked phenomenon which has been documented since the 1950s.

It has been shown that there is a strong correlation between inadequate induction and early leavers, and that the latter is not only found in times of full employment. Even in recessions, new recruits make up the highest proportion of the total numbers leaving.

How quickly they leave will depend largely on the type of work. White collar workers tend to stay up to a year or two 'because it looks better on their CV'. The *decision* to leave has usually been taken very early on. Unskilled workers will often leave earlier. Surveys in the 1950s showed that 40–50 per cent of the workers had less than three months' service.

If you want to reduce the labour turnover in your organisation, it follows that tackling the problem of early leavers will pay dividends. Monitor your induction programme against the figures for labour turnover and the new employee survival index. (Chapter 8 addresses this in more detail.)

Most of the costs of employing staff (with the exception of ongoing salary costs and some training investment) are incurred at the front end, ie the investment is made in terms of the initial recruitment and training and there is a delay before the return on this investment becomes evident, when the employee is working effectively and productively.

The cost of this initial high staff turnover can be huge:

- cost of advertising
- cost of recruitment and selection (including interviewer's time, etc)
- cost of temporary replacement
- loss of output during the period of the vacancy (few employers manage to replace their staff before the present incumbent has left, even where long notice periods exist)
- salary costs of the new person
- cost of low output and high supervision requirements in initial period
- often low morale and productivity of subordinates and peers.

Once all these costs have been borne, if the new starter leaves, costs are incurred all over again. For employees on high salaries, the costs can be very high indeed, as they are often proportionate to the salary.

It may be difficult to find another replacement, too. In choosing the preferred candidate, the organisation will probably have rejected other good ones, who may now have been snapped up by competitors. Interested applicants may be suspicious about the job if the last incumbent obviously found it so intolerable that their tenure was so short.

In addition, few people who leave jobs quickly feel that it is their fault. In many cases they will blame the company, feeling that the job was oversold and did not match up to the rosy expectations they had generated after the interview. They will complain to their friends and the image of the company suffers, possibly affecting the customer base.

High staff turnover can cause productivity to decrease and recruitment and training costs to escalate as new recruits must be found and brought up to effectiveness. If senior managers do not become effective quickly or if they leave early, this can affect the company's financial situation.

Studies have shown that early leaving is reduced by an initial intensive training period. Research in America in the 1950s and 1960s showed that a short booklet, designed to reduce unrealistic expectations about the job, reduced labour turnover even when given after the recruits had made the decision to join (but before they arrived). Orientation and adjustment can begin before the first day.

It should be noted that although induction is important, it cannot counteract the negative effects of bad recruitment.

Common causes of early leaving

There are a number of causes cited when people are asked why they left a job earlier than they would have hoped:

- False expectations
- Company style
- Demands of the job
- Difficulty with colleagues.

False expectations of the new job

The most common cause of early leaving is false expectations of the job. Overselling during the recruitment process means that the job may not turn out to be what the new recruit thought it would be. This can arise from glowing but inaccurate descriptions focusing on the unusual aspects of the job, or where the proportion of time spent on various activities within the job is quite different from the impression given by the coverage on the job description.

Another aspect of overselling the job is misunderstanding about salary or promotion prospects. Interviewers often give estimates of approximately how long an individual would be expected to wait before a pay rise or promotion, but may err on the positive side because they want to be encouraging. In some companies there is a great difference between what is said, eg 'We promote on merit', and what is seen to happen, eg colleagues disabuse the newcomer of any idea of promotion on the grounds that three old hands are 'in the queue' first.

If earnings are quoted including overtime pay, the new recruit will assume that the overtime is readily available.

There are many instances of individuals feeling that they have been promised a pay rise or a company car, etc, after six months or 'when they've proved themselves', without any such detail being part of the employment contract. The individual waits, hopes and then leaves in disillusion.

The induction process should strengthen the favourable attitudes and impressions which newcomers have taken on during the recruitment and selection process, emphasise the reality of the job, and gradually counteract any overselling that has been done.

Company style

Although new recruits can assume a certain amount from the wording of the job advertisement, the company style and culture may come as a surprise. They may find too much or too little bureaucracy and control. (The latter is not so uncommon; it can be very comforting to have the security of rules and regulations for some, so that people know exactly what they can and cannot do.)

New starters need help to adjust to different cultures, formal or informal, typical of large or small companies or of long-established family firms or zany go-ahead newcomers, etc.

Demands of the job

In some cases, particularly if adequate training is not given, or if the individual has oversold their own skills, the demands of the job may prove too great. This is often the case in bad promotions, where the individual was very successful at the job below but where the skills needed for the new job may be entirely different. Many successful sales representatives make poor sales managers, for instance, as the skills required are different.

Alternatively, the job may turn out to be too easy – particularly if the brightest recruit was chosen without due thought as to how long the job would keep them absorbed.

Difficulty with colleagues

Personality clashes are more common where the new person has not met the boss or colleagues as part of the recruitment process. The importance of group dynamics cannot be underestimated, and the individual will be under a lot of subtle pressure to 'fit in' with the group.

Personality clashes, particularly with the immediate manager or supervisor, may be difficult to pin down as many people prefer to cite other reasons for leaving rather than admitting that they did not feel comfortable with their workmates. They may not admit the real reason even to themselves, as vague feelings and their sense of unease are often confused and unsubstantiated, so justifying their leaving with something more tangible, such as better pay elsewhere, is seen as being more acceptable, politer and involves less self-questioning.

Probationary period and termination

There is another big cost of ineffective induction (or recruitment) – that of having to dismiss the employee. It has been said that the cost of this is rather less, though, than that of keeping an employee who is less than effective. Discontented employees are unlikely to be effective. They can cause problems with colleagues, spreading negativity, interrupting their work or becoming isolated and stand-offish. They may have high fault or error rates in their work, creating a high scrap or waste rate and requiring work to be repeated, with the consequent use of extra resources and time. In severe cases, they can eventually cause industrial relations difficulties from these problems.

If an employee's performance is not adequate, new management may weed them out later, but this is much more costly and damaging to the individual and to the company. There are opportunity costs, too, of all the opportunities missed owing to poor performance, which would have been seized by better staff. It is easier and fairer to part company early on rather than prolonging the process.

Many managers worry about dismissal, being scared of firing somebody or feeling guilty about it. They may need support and reassurance to show them that they are acting in the best interests of the company and that it is hardly fair to prolong the period when the employee is struggling.

However, the purpose of the probationary period is positive. It allows the manager to monitor the individual's progress and help them to get up to speed as quickly as possible – in general, people want to feel that they are doing their job. During the probationary period, both the employee and the organisation are on trial, each evaluating the other. This does not have to be threatening for the individual; the employer can re-emphasise the fact that they chose that employee, often after considerable selection processes or testing.

Even with the best of motives, a new and inexperienced person can be disruptive to 'old hands' who find it unsettling having to explain and justify everything. They may feel threatened by new ideas, or they may worry whether the new person will fit into the team or 'rock the boat'. This is doubly emphasised if the new person is the boss! So, the sooner the new person is integrated, the better it is for everyone concerned.

What is induction?

The induction process covers any and all arrangements made to familiarise the new employee with the organisation, safety rules, general conditions of employment and the work of the section or department in which they are employed. It includes everything from the very mundane (but very important), such as where to find paper and pens, to imparting a sophisticated understanding of the business.

Good induction should follow on from good recruitment and selection, and will involve the initial welcome, on-the-job training, acclimatisation and often a formal induction course. It is the responsibility of management to ensure that the individual has the information and guidance needed to succeed. After the individuals themselves, it is the immediate manager who has the greatest interest in ensuring that the new starter has settled in quickly and effectively.

Good induction should:

- help to define performance expectations
- speed up the response to work training
- maintain the motivation of newcomers and a commitment to organisational goals
- for promotees, it should instil a desire to succeed at the same or a higher level than the one they previously achieved
- foster good working habits
- increase productivity earlier
- reduce performance problems
- reduce error rate
- reduce the numbers of early leavers
- reduce absenteeism
- lead to better customer service (once their own needs are catered for, they can cater for the needs of others)

- improve employee morale and enhance positive attitudes
- improve manager/subordinate relationships, and lay the foundations for mutual respect
- develop sense of belonging and satisfaction with the organisation
- improve understanding of company policies, procedures and rules
- improve understanding of company benefits
- develop and maintain an acceptable conformity to the formal and informal rules of dress and behaviour, etc.

Good induction should also help managers to spot recruitment mistakes early and to highlight further training needs. It should help to avoid new employees having to say, 'I didn't know I was supposed to do it like that'. It should reduce or remove the series of other small frustrations as new recruits are relieved of their initial uncertainties. It allows a more accurate assessment of newcomers and permits the company to harness their skills and experience through creating a safe but stimulating learning environment.

Who should be given induction training?

There are many categories of workers who will benefit from induction or re-induction training: new recruits to the company, people who have transferred jobs or been promoted (but are already in the company), expatriates and returning expatriates and in some cases even long-term temporary workers, depending on how long they are likely to stay.

Induction training should be available for all grades (suitably tailored) and all functions of workers, from the top to the bottom of the organisation. Special needs for specific categories of workers are dealt with in Chapter 6.

Contents of an induction programme

Traditionally there are two parts to induction: the personnel inputs – forms, talking about organisational values, etc – and the information and instructions given by the immediate manager or supervisor, ie the introduction to work, explanation of general policies, relationship between this job and others and physical setting, etc.

Induction must be structured, plans need to be written and checked for omissions so that nothing is overlooked. It is not just a course or a handshake tour, although it usually includes fairly informal inputs. Often a checklist is used so that progress can be checked and the manager can monitor what information and training have been given, and when. Sections can be ticked off as they are completed.

Details of company products are likely to be forgotten if given on the first day, because of the mass of new information the new recruit is receiving and the initial anxieties. Information should be prioritised so that newcomers learn the most important parts early on. This can be grouped to cover:

- What newcomers *must* know, eg safety requirements
- What they *should* know, eg how to do their job, and how to find their way around, and
- What they *could* know, eg company products, history, etc.

The company can then decide how to break this down, and what information to give before joining, on the first day, in the first week, the first months and during the probationary period. The best programmes give the newcomers plenty of time, structuring the inputs over several weeks or months. Integration with the organisation requires a degree of attitudinal change in many cases, which cannot be accomplished overnight.

Induction should be tailored to the individual. It should be appropriate to the grade of the recruit, the sophistication or complexity of the job, and to the previous experience of the individual. It must be systematic and must fulfil the needs of the new starters. This can often be achieved by asking them what they think they need.

The length of the induction period, and correspondingly the probationary period, should be related to the length of the learning curve. If the details of the job can be quickly learned because they are relatively simple and repetitive, the induction can be completed more quickly than if the job is complex, involves making subjective judgements, or is such that some duties are undertaken only at certain periods during the year and cannot be learned earlier.

Induction in smaller companies will generally take less time than in larger ones, and will finish earlier as there is comparatively less new information for the new recruit to assimilate in terms of the company, the people and probably the job.

Is induction worth the cost and effort?

The initial training of new recruits is not without cost. It uses a lot of supervisory time, together with the cost of informal and formal training. However, it is not just a question of kindness but makes good business sense. It does not have to be expensive and, if the individual is retained, the return on the investment will have been made. Ineffective induction, or a lack of it, can cost a great deal more.

A good induction programme demonstrates to the individual the investment of time and money in them, and the interest in them. People need to see that they are important when they join a new company, not just as a walking set of skills but as the individuals they are. This aids their adjustment into the company and the job, instilling pride in the company and satisfying their need to belong. Most people want to belong, to be accepted as members of a group. Engendering a feeling of belonging to the company develops commitment to organisational goals. The employer then maximises the retention and contribution of the workforce and gets a faster return on investments. In addition, enthusiastic recruits can be great 'sales representatives' for the company.

It must be noted that good induction is not a panacea for all other organisational evils. It can only be really effective when building on good personnel policies and recruitment and selection practices. If the organisation does not attract and select the right staff, induction cannot magically change them into super-employees. The organisation must look at all its personnel policies to ensure that they attract, motivate, reward and retain the right people. Induction will undoubtedly help in the retention of staff and their motivation providing that it is congruent with the other elements of employment.

Chapter 2

The Behavioural Contract

Employees should be provided with a formal contract of employment, giving details of their terms and conditions, within 13 weeks. In addition, a strong informal and unwritten contract emerges and it is this which determines employees' behaviour and productivity.

Organisations put a great deal of effort into the recruitment and selection processes, undertaking job analyses, compiling job descriptions, testing for skills, experience and other attributes against person specifications, and creating objectives and standards for employees to measure up to.

However, at some time between entry to the organisation and the first anniversary, many employees slither into the 'lost workforce'. They have either left the company, or have learned to survive in the company while doing the bare minimum. The perceptions of their managers are that they have simply not realised their potential, or that they were just not motivated enough to do the job.

The term 'presenteeism' is sometimes used to describe those who attend their jobs in body but not mind. This may manifest itself when the individual has already taken the decision to leave the company as soon as decently possible, or can go hand in hand with a decision to 'time-serve' – picking up the pay cheque without feeling a personal need to contribute. This phenomenon can grow like a cancer if a number of employees feel dispirited and may be more difficult to combat than absenteeism, where a distinct problem is easier to identify. Both are costly to the employer.

It has been said that most people make the decision to stay or leave in the first two weeks, so the information imparted during this time is crucially important.

In various ways, options about how to behave in the organisation are presented to the newcomer, often in methods scarcely suspected by the management. The formal employment contract presents one aspect of the choices. It states that the employee shall work for *x* hours a day, for *x* hours per week, with meal breaks, etc as specified. It implies that employees shall expend effort and try to do their best at all times, and it often specifies the methods by which they will be judged.

The formal organisation espouses the structure of the work, the work environment and stated relationships. The behavioural contract adopted by the new recruit, and endorsed by the immediate line manager, may be quite different. Many variables influence the new starter (and other employees too – the initial contract is under constant review and liable to revision) as part of the socialisation process. The new recruit assimilates the sometimes conflicting messages from all sources, and then makes the judgement and decision on how far they will go to compromise.

One of the major influences is the behaviour of the 'human organisation', ie bosses, colleagues, fellow workers and subordinates. Although the organisation may be able to identify and publicise preferred role models, the new employee will attach much more relevance to those closest at hand. Where the individual perceives some incongruence between the stated requirements of the job and their observations on how activity in the workplace matches them, a personal decision is made on how they will react to the expectations of the new organisation, ie they deduce exactly what will and will not be tolerated or approved of. This means that they will watch their closest associates before deciding how they should behave.

In synopsis, the newcomers ask themselves:

What are the stated rules?
Are my associates working to them?
Do I want to accept them?

The organisation has given them recipes both for their own action and schemes for interpreting the actions of others.

Once the individual has decided on a mode of behaviour and an acceptable level of performance, their personal and psychological contract is made and they will perform in a manner consistent with it. The decision hinges on the impressions the new starter has gained in terms of what is *expected* and what is *accepted*.

Organisationally controlled influences include:

- the interview, recruitment literature and advertisement, etc
- the formal orientation process
- job training
- supervision given.

Factors outside the organisation's control include:

- initial observations by the new starter
- the newcomer's perceptions of others' behaviour
- the personal needs of the new recruit, which influence the contents of the informal contract.

'Culture' is dynamic rather than static. The new employee can influence it as well as be influenced by it. As the newcomer judges the organisation, so the organisation will also judge the newcomer from the impact of the first few days.

The concept of culture is elusive and easily misunderstood. Consequently, the induction process is not as straightforward as it may initially appear. On an induction course the trainer puts forward their view of the company, coloured by their perceptions. Others may see this slightly differently. Words used may have particular connotations to individuals depending on their past experience. However, despite difficulties there are many positive steps that organisations can take, and knowledge of the factors involved can only help:

- Company literature
- The impact of the interview
- The supervisor's influence
- Peer pressure
- The psychological contract.

Company literature

Company literature has a major influence on the way in which the newcomer perceives the organisation. Visual images used in the advertisement portray a vision of the company as do the words chosen. These give subtle information on the culture of the company. The organisation may be perceived as formal if people are referred to by title, eg 'Please reply in writing to Mr Johnson' or informal if forenames are used and writing seems less important, eg 'Please ring John on ... for more details'.

The images the company uses to portray itself create visions and perceptions about it. The organisational history may be described in terms of its growth – from birth through to maturity. The action of the company may be described in terms of 'fighting the competition' and 'winning', etc. These create the impression of an aggressive 'go-getting' army of people determined and united in their objectives. The newcomer may be greeted in terms that convey the feeling of becoming part of one large family. Company information on entrepreneurial managers and risk-taking business venturers may contrast with and be diluted by exhortations for hard work, suggestions of long hours of work and disapproval of those 'rocking the boat'.

Recruitment literature should be congruent with literature given on induction and later in the individual's career. It should also relate to what they actually experience. Welcome letters that 'hope' the newcomers will look forward to a 'rewarding career' with the organisation will carry little weight with people recruited to undertake boring, routine production line jobs which are known to offer few future prospects.

Information given by the company will be supplemented by the opinions of friends and family, each potentially altering the individual's perception of the organisation and/or the job.

The impact of the interview

The period of socialisation begins early, with the new recruit's first contact with the company. The recruitment process can be seen as a public relations exercise. People invariably believe that what is seen at the interview is typical of the company as a whole. This may or may not be true; the interviewer(s) may be trying very hard to show the company or the job in a better light than it really is.

The behaviour of the interviewer is fundamentally important as it shapes the expectations built up for the future. It has been found that non-verbal cues, ie the unspoken signals conveyed, have a greater impact than verbal ones.

Non-verbal behaviour includes:

- facial expressions
- eyes and eye movements
- hand movements and gestures
- body movements and posture
- distance between individuals.

It seems that, without necessarily being able to describe how they do it, people make judgements and form impressions based on non-verbal indicators, such as the physical proximity of the other individual and how they move and gesticulate. These judgements can be made very quickly, within the first few seconds of meeting, and the individuals then subconsciously test out the assumptions made throughout the interview.

Research has shown that, while watching someone, the impact of the message is more than half made up by the appearance of the individual, with only a small percentage coming from what they say and rather more from how they say it. So a job applicant will look first at what the interviewer's body is saying to them, then how the voice is pitched, and only lastly the content of what they say. This is obviously true of all situations, not just interviews. Most of us will have watched someone saying something about a friend or colleague, while looking upwards, eyes shrugged to the ceiling. The vocal message is completely and comprehensively contradicted by the visual information. So, if the interviewer, or later a colleague, says something which is contradicted by their body language, the verbal message is negated.

The more people who interview or meet the applicant at the recruitment and selection stage, the more likely it is that the newcomer will build realistic impressions.

The supervisor's influence

The attitude of the immediate boss is very important. The newcomer watches the boss's behaviour towards their bosses, towards their job and towards others. They observe the team to see how much challenge to the leader is tolerated, and whether the team talk about their managers disrespectfully. They watch to see how much time the boss makes for others (and for them). They notice whether their colleagues jump to attention when the boss enters. All these influences are powerful; new recruits want to be approved of, but they need to keep their job, which is in the gift of their immediate line manager, who will recommend their further employment, or not.

There may also be conspicuous incongruence between the stated objectives of equality and single status and the practice of hierarchical management, an all-powerful boss or blatant status-consciousness. All this becomes apparent to the motivated watcher; newcomers absorb every piece of information so that they can assimilate the realities and act accordingly.

Peer pressure

Intentionally or not, the behaviour of the new starter's associates will influence them. The company has to rely on its workforce to project a good image which upholds their core values. Even if it attempts to monitor this through performance appraisal, etc, it is largely out of their control. If the workforce is demoralised, this can quickly rub off on the newcomer and makes it very hard for them to keep their initial enthusiasm. The more positive colleagues seem, as demonstrated by what they *do* rather than what they *say*, the easier the newcomer will find it to adapt to the new working environment.

New starters notice evidence of pride in the organisation and the cheerfulness and apparent satisfaction (or not) of the workers. Even such evidence as the jokes told can be taken into account. This can then be reinforced or contradicted by organisational information, such as company notice boards and posters.

The influence of group pressure should not be underestimated. Human beings are social animals with strong needs to belong. Their worst deprivation is separation and loss of contact with others (which is why being ignored or 'sent to Coventry' is such a powerful weapon). In some organisations practical jokes are routinely played on newcomers as part of their 'rites of passage' into the group. The trials and tests of apprenticeships are well documented, but the practice does not only affect young workers. The more different the individual is seen to be from the rest of the group, the more this usually occurs.

The purposes of such practices or initiations, be they subtle or deliberate and obvious, are to test the newcomer so that the group can decide if they are competent and whether to admit them to the group. They are often seen as enormous fun and brighten up the day in otherwise monotonous working conditions. Dangerous jokes, where risks of injury are great, are often played in environments where the group may later have to rely on the expertise of the newcomer for the safety of all. Dangerous jokes are designed to alert newcomers to danger and to ensure speedy learning.

Inducing the feeling of being an outsider, the butt of practical jokes, increases the individual's desire to be accepted by the group. It also establishes the newcomer's place in the hierarchy and ensures continuity of existing group practices. When the newcomer is no longer perceived as a threat they will be admitted to the group. Alternatively, if practical jokes continue, newcomers may leave.

There are also many documented cases where individuals have been sacked for working too fast, or for exposing fraud or inadequacy in their workmates. In less extreme instances, the newcomer is persuaded to 'toe the line' with breaches of the rules.

For example, alcohol may be frowned on and the company may have a 'dry' policy, including rules that staff must not operate machinery after drinking or will be sent home if they smell of alcohol. If everyone in the newcomer's department, including the boss, spends two hours in the local pub on Friday lunchtimes, it is hard for them not to join in and difficult for them to retain belief in company rules.

Another example of peer pressure is the common practice of fiddling company expenses. Although the new recruit is often anxious to please and keen to abide by the rules, if all the 'old hands' claim a few 'little extras', the recruit may be subjected to a 'friendly chat' and offered the advice that if they don't play the game they will ruin it for everybody.

The difficulty for the newcomer is that the conduct which goes against all that they have been told appears to be condoned formally, often from high in the organisation.

If there is a gulf between the organisation's stated values and those perceived from the behaviour and conduct of their associates, new employees will begin to feel uncomfortable, particularly if, as in the examples above, they could theoretically be disciplined for their 'offences'. They may take the decision to leave the company, mentally or physically.

Influencing the psychological contract

The integration process can be influenced positively or negatively. The employee joins, or accepts promotion or whatever, willing and ready to be accepted and to perform well. They will do their best to fit in, if only because it is more comfortable for them that way.

If communication lines with the immediate supervisor, and perhaps their managers, are honest and open, the manager can begin to decipher what messages have been picked up. Once that information filters in, managers can take steps to reinforce or counteract the messages as appropriate. Knowledge of group dynamics will aid the manager – the newcomer will inevitably disrupt group patterns to some extent and the manager will benefit from an understanding of the techniques of teambuilding.

Taking psychological factors into account will help the organisation to harness and sustain the enthusiasm of new starters. Most begin with high hopes, aiming to increase the effectiveness and efficiency of the organisation, to contribute fully and to achieve personal satisfaction. They may well hope for an increase in salary when they achieve all this too!

Although it will evidently be preferable to maintain the early goodwill of the newcomer, if they have got off on the wrong foot remedies are possible. First impressions are lasting and not easy to erase, but they can be altered. The psychological contract is effectively monitored and reviewed and adjustments to it can be made if the people or surroundings change. Someone who has made up their mind to leave can alter their opinions if the messages are changed.

Keeping newcomers motivated

The seriousness and speed with which instructions and guidance are presented will show the newcomer to what extent they have to be followed. Flippancy and haste will detract from the message, and the new recruit will believe that only lip service is paid to them. If job training is given too hurriedly, the newcomer will assume that quality and standards are relatively unimportant and not something worth taking time over. If the individual is told that high performance and output are required, but sees peers and colleagues doing rather less, the conclusion will be that they can do as they please.

Avoid making promises, or anything that could be taken as a commitment, if they cannot be kept. If the promised car or promotion does not materialise when the new employee thought it would, their performance and commitment to the organisation will suffer. Ensure that any such details are clearly explained with the letter offering them the job, and again when they first join, to avoid misunderstandings.

If they discover that promotion is not actually on merit, or does not appear that way, they are likely to become cynical about other statements made by the company.

The organisational practice of rewards and recognition must also reinforce desired behaviour. If newcomers see peers and colleagues doing rather less than they should, and getting bonuses or higher pay, the effect will be that they will do as they please.

The induction programme

Perceptions about how the company runs will also be gained from the induction process and how any formal inputs or course is run. For example, if an induction course is common to all grades, and participants come from different areas of the company, this will reinforce statements about minimising hierarchical differences and working as one company-wide team.

Information comes to the new recruit from a vast number and variety of sources. Their congruence with the organisational message underpins their credibility. If the informal inputs do not concur, this will cast doubt on each new company message received, making it harder to counteract damage done early on.

Although it may seem to be outside the organisation's scope to influence the individual's personal needs, which also help to shape the psychological contract, these may be investigated during thorough testing and probing interviews. Candidates selected should then be those whose personal needs most closely match the organisational ones.

It should be emphasised that the aim of induction is not absolute conformity or the creation of clones, but to produce individuals who function effectively in the organisation, without necessarily accepting every aspect in its entirety.

Chapter 3

Pre-employment Preparation

The induction process begins during recruitment and selection. First impressions about the company are formed at this stage. Good recruitment literature will mean that a number of the new employee's questions will already have been answered. However, there will be many others, and there are several important areas to attend to before the newcomer arrives at the company on the first day. These are divided into information that should be provided to the new recruit before joining, and the 'behind the scenes' activities to be undertaken to ensure that the initial period goes smoothly.

Pre-employment information

The offer letter

This is the first formal contact with the individual after the recruitment and selection phase. Even if the post has been offered to them in a telephone conversation, most recruits will want to wait for the formal offer before handing in their notice in their current job.

It is normal for the offer to congratulate the recipient; the point is to prove that after a possibly lengthy and rigorous selection process the organisation is very pleased to have found them.

The offer should contain details covering:

- the post offered, job title and brief description of responsibilities, etc
- the starting date (this may have been discussed, but can naturally be varied by mutual consent)
- the starting salary or wage, and any other financial benefits
- salary progressions (when and how much, etc), if appropriate
- the rate or method of calculating pay, and the intervals at which it will be paid
- the grade of the job, and what that means
- basic terms and conditions, such as hours of work (including breaks), holidays (including public holiday entitlements and accrued holiday pay on leaving), sickness (sick leave and pay), pension arrangements (or that no pension arrangements exist, and whether or not a contracting-out certificate was issued under the Social Security Pensions Act 1975), etc
- the location of the post (or head office, if the job is mobile)

- relocation package and details, if applicable
- the probationary period
- any other material factors.

The offer should make it clear whether it is conditional upon satisfactory references or medical checks, etc. If a medical is required, you should tell the newcomer whether this will be paid for but should be arranged by them, or whether it will necessitate a visit to the company occupational health unit (where care should be taken not to expect them to 'know the ropes' or treat them 'like a number'), etc. A specimen job offer letter is given on page 39.

Where elements of the package are negotiable, it is usual to reach agreement in a telephone conversation before putting the offer in writing. Where particular conditions apply, these should be clear. For example, in many organisations a trade union may have negotiating rights so that salary or wages are determined by this method, rather than through individual negotiation. If the individual is liable for transfer, or a mobility clause is included, this should be made clear. It is advisable not to make the job description part of the terms and conditions of the post, as this makes changes to it more difficult in the future. If you need flexibility in hours or place of work, the offer and contract should specify this in order to avoid complications and misunderstandings later.

The formal offer should give individuals all the details they need to assess the offer fairly, and to decide whether to accept. If joining instructions are not enclosed with this letter, they should be sent separately on acceptance.

A formal written contract of employment does not have to be included at this stage, but a statement of the main terms and conditions is important so that the individual understands what the contract means. This statement has the status of a legal document, so it is advisable to have it professionally produced.

A contract is legally in existence as soon as the employee accepts an offer of work in return for pay. A written contract need not be provided until 13 weeks. It does not have to go into detail but should contain:

- the names of the employer and employee
- the date for continuous service
- the periods of notice on either side (which must be equal to or greater than the statutory minimum)
- the job title of the person to whom grievances should be addressed

as well as those items on the list specified for the offer letter (above), eg hours of work, salary, starting date, etc. The description of the probationary period should say whether or not this can be extended if performance is not quite up to standard by the end. It should say how the performance will be judged and perhaps what interim reports are to be made. It should be made clear that the company will not wait until the end of the period to dismiss any individual if there is sufficient reason before, such as unsatisfactory performance or conduct.

There are also implied terms to the contract which do not have to be specifically written in. These are deemed implications of all employment contracts. They include requirements for the employee to:

- maintain trust and confidence through co-operation
- act in good faith towards the company
- take reasonable care to ensure health and safety in the workplace.

Full details of statutory rights are not given here, but the employer must ensure that these are understood and adhere to them.

First day instructions

Once the job has been accepted in writing the newcomer can be sent instructions for the first day. These should include reporting details such as:

- where to report to, ie which building on the site, the exact location inside the building, along with a map of how to get there if this is complex, which entrance of the building to use if there is more than one, etc
- who to report to – the person's name and job title
- when to report – the starting time for new employees is often later than normal, so that whoever is meeting them has time to deal with urgent matters and to prepare. The date can also be clarified to avoid any confusion.

It is also helpful to tell individuals how to get there (public transport routes, etc) if the work location is different from the interview one, and to give information on where they can park if using their own transport, enclosing a car parking permit if appropriate.

New starters should be informed of any meetings or commitments made on their behalf during their first couple of weeks, particularly if these will involve encroaching on their leisure time (which is not advisable if it can be avoided).

This letter should also tell them what to bring with them when they arrive, for instance:

- the P45 employment form or National Insurance number
- SSP forms
- their bank or building society details (so that they can be paid)
- birth certificate
- certificates of qualifications
- work permit
- driving licence, etc.

Companies sometimes ask to see important documents before the employee joins. Research has shown that about 10 per cent of job applicants exaggerate their qualifications so many employers check on this.

The letter should enclose any forms to be signed and returned, such as commercial or Official Secrets documents, etc not already completed. It should also ask the individual for certain information before joining, such as clothes size for uniforms, etc and perhaps whether they have any holidays already booked, so that appropriate arrangements can be made.

The employer may also wish to offer help with relocation and finding accommodation if the new employee has to move home. If a full relocation package is to be offered, the newcomer should be given details as early as possible.

The 'welcome pack'

Many companies send new starters a 'welcome pack' which contains more information on the company together with contractual details (if these have not already been sent with the letter offering the job) and a welcome letter signed by the immediate supervisor, or everyone in the department. Welcome packs can also contain:

- a welcome letter from the company chairperson or managing director
- hierarchy charts, showing job titles and names, to help newcomers understand where they fit in and to familiarise them with their new colleagues' names
- details of rules and conditions of service (if not given before)
- a welcome letter from the recognised trade union or staff association.

Although the recruitment literature will have been useful, there may be other pieces of company information that you now wish to provide. For instance, the recruit may now be trusted to become privy to confidential information which they would not have been given access to before. There may also be further detailed literature describing the organisation.

Information should be geared to what the jobholder is likely to want and find interesting. For instance, it would be unusual to provide an unskilled worker with the last annual report and interim financial statements, whereas a senior manager would expect it.

Where it is crucial that company values are embraced immediately, information about them may be sent. These items often include literature on customer care or quality and what that means for the company and its employees. It can also cover the religious, political or philosophical stance of the organisation, where there is one, though this will usually have been obvious throughout the selection process.

The immediate supervisor or manager may also wish to suggest suitable reading for some categories of recruits, while making it clear that this is not compulsory. The volume of new information should be kept to reasonable levels – nobody appreciates heavy tomes.

You may also wish to extend an invitation to visit the workplace for a half-day so that the newcomer can get to know some of the people and something of the job in advance. It is particularly useful to meet the new boss if he or she will not be around on the individual's first day at work, or if the two have not met during the recruitment process. It is important for the newcomer to see the workspace too – jobs have been turned down because of the thought of working in smoke-filled rooms – it is obviously better for both parties if newcomers have time to begin to adjust to the new surroundings before they start.

Behind the scenes

The line manager must prepare for the newcomer's first day. Whatever is planned in terms of later formal induction programmes is immaterial if the first day was unplanned and, as has been discussed, the new starter does not come back for the second day.

Organising the work

Some thought should be given to what the new employee will *do* on the first day. Although a lot of time may be spent in initial introductions, talking to people and completing necessary paperwork, the newcomer should be given some *meaningful* work, not just reams of undifferentiated reading. Plan the work that they will be given so that the common practice of giving only menial tasks is avoided. Where reading matter is given, this can be broken down into what is needed immediately, and how much more (after all the pre-arrival reading) the individual is expected to be able to digest.

It may be useful to ask the last incumbent or a fellow worker to leave notes about the job for the new person. These should give the very basic, 'nuts and bolts' details needed initially, such as contact phone numbers, who to ask for help about which aspects of work, etc, and the peaks and troughs of the job. If the last incumbent is being promoted, it may be possible for them to be released for short periods now and then to help in the training of the new jobholder, but their new boss will have to be approached too. (A balance must be struck, however, particularly if the organisation wants fresh ideas from taking on 'new blood'. Too much time spent with the last jobholder during the initial period will tend to mitigate against fresh ideas and instil a 'you-do-it-this-way' mentality, as old habits become ingrained in the new person.)

Thought must also be given to what the manager will do on the newcomer's first day. Allocate and diarise sufficient time in the first week.

Briefing colleagues

Other staff and colleagues should be briefed about the new recruit – in most cases they will be curious, and not unconcerned about what impact the newcomer will have on them. They can also be part of the welcome if they know who the new person is and expect them.

It can be useful to set up a few introductory meetings during the first week, so that the newcomer meets colleagues early on but without being swamped, and so that the other employees know that they will see the new person before they have had a full description through the office grapevine.

If the immediate supervisor or manager will not be around on the newcomer's first day, the new recruit should be warned in advance. If possible, a meeting should be arranged before the newcomer starts – even more imperative if the two have not met before. The manager should explain why they will not be there and apologise. If they are on holiday, this will be seen as legitimate by the newcomer. If the manager is away on a course, or attending an important meeting, the newcomer must be reassured that the manager expects to spend time with them in future. The newcomer should be told who will see them and look after them on their first day(s) and what the manager will do on returning to the office.

Administrative arrangements

The importance of making sure that the office is ready for the newcomer's arrival should not be underestimated. Not everyone goes as far as providing flowers (though this unusual touch is very welcoming and is often much appreciated), but there are obvious items of equipment, etc which should be provided in advance. The new recruit should not have to go searching for stationery and equipment. Keys and passcards should be ready for them, and security access to building areas or computers, etc should have been authorised in advance.

The work area should be ready for occupation, so if another member of staff has left, it should be cleared of any remaining personal effects. If the desk or locker has been empty for a while, it should be thoroughly cleaned. The individual should have some workspace, a desk or locker or whatever, to call their own. (Although these details seem very basic, not all employers seem to think of them.)

Door nameplates and business cards, etc should be ordered (and preferably delivered) if they are to be provided, showing the name by which the individual wishes to be known. This means that the newcomer can be effective in meeting people early on rather than finding that potential customers forget who they are and where they come from. The impact of arranging all this in advance will be lost if the nameplate is wrong. If it arrives saying 'Elizabeth Smart', but the newcomer has been known by her second name, Jane, since birth, or always uses an abbreviation of her name, she will feel uncomfortable rather than impressed.

Training

Consider what training the newcomer will need. Essential job training and any formal induction course should be booked in advance, so that the employer can give details, dates and times of the training when the new recruit arrives. It may be useful to check possible dates first if the employee is joining in a peak holiday period.

Some organisations arrange a paid training day for new starters before they join, or give them an initial training before they start the job properly. (This often happens if there are safety needs, and untrained staff cannot be allowed into the work area.) In the latter situation the group completes all the necessary paperwork and then begins job training. The course will also include all the elements they need to know immediately, such as fire procedures, and full induction, with talks on company history and ethos, products, customers and suppliers, and terms and conditions and rules.

This may also be a good time to review the supervisor's training, giving refresher training on induction if required. Checklists can be given to remind them of the importance of induction, what to include in the programme, how to train and how to link this to material given on any formal induction course.

Managers and supervisors need to be trained in the necessary skills for induction, as the personnel specialist or trainer cannot sprint between departments each time a new recruit has to be trained. It is the supervisor's responsibility to give most of the information and co-workers should not be relied on to give adequate or accurate information without checking.

It is useful for supervisors to remember how long it took them to get to know their way around and to share that information. A thorough airing of the first-day jitters can remind the old stalwarts what it felt like to be the new person at work and may help to convince them of the need for good orientation. In addition, they can be asked to say what *they* would like if they were going to a new job, so that they can act accordingly towards the newcomer.

If they are to give on-the-job training to the new starter they should be formally instructed on how to go about this, and on the need for structured inputs and training in manageable chunks. There are many good books on this topic (some are recommended at the end of this book – see pages 155–157) so the details are omitted here.

Role of personnel

The personnel department, or other managers who fulfil the personnel role, have many 'behind the scenes' tasks to perform, both before the new recruits arrive and after.

Personnel's role includes:

- telling managers the starting dates of new people well in advance
- sending joining information, greeting individuals and dealing with the initial documentation
- designing the timetable and administering formal induction training

- training supervisors on how to train and give induction
- issuing checklists for supervisors and giving guidance, eg on choosing buddies (see page 56)
- monitoring appraisals, and checking that they are taking place
- co-ordinating subsequent or associated training for newcomers as training needs are identified
- providing a welfare and counselling service
- advising on difficult probation and dismissal cases
- monitoring the induction process, formal and informal (evaluating it and collecting statistics on leavers, etc)
- providing budgets for induction to ensure that it happens
- designing, reviewing and amending the induction policy.

The induction policy

As mentioned, it will be the responsibility of the personnel department to draw up and monitor any induction policy. The policy should include:

(a) Senior management commitment, demonstrated by:

- the signature of senior manager(s)
- a rule or commitment that new starters will always be released for any formal off-the-job induction training (except in exceptional circumstances)
- a commitment that senior managers will attend parts of the induction course and give presentations as appropriate
- the provision of a budget for induction training for new starters and appraisal and performance monitoring training, etc for supervisors and managers.

(b) Details of the induction course:

- the name of the person responsible for organising, co-ordinating or overseeing induction training (formal and informal)
- the time limit by which the new starters should have received any formal off-the-job induction training (eg normally within two months of their starting date)
- a definition of who should be eligible for induction courses, eg that this should not cover only new employees, but also promotees
- a broad outline of what should be included in the induction course (and perhaps how this should differ for different groups of inductees to cater for their special needs)
- a commitment to evaluating and updating the induction course (by a named person/job title).

(c) Details of on-the-job or job skills training (minima to be provided)

(d) Commitment to provide all the information and equipment necessary and the names or job titles of the people responsible for organising this and deciding what is appropriate

(e) Commitments on follow-up and performance monitoring:

- all new starters should be given regular appraisals during their probationary period (number and/or timings can be specified)
- responsibility for on-the-job induction training, arranging further appropriate training and undertaking regular performance monitoring to be included in the job descriptions of all managers
- decisions on whether an employee will be made permanent, have their probation extended or be dismissed should be taken before the end of the probationary period, and this will be discussed with them
- policy that probationary periods should only be extended in exceptional circumstances, with the agreement of the person responsible for induction, and limits on the duration of any extension.

(f) Commitments on training to be given to supervisors and first-line managers:

- all supervisors and managers should be trained in basic induction techniques
- supervisors and managers should be trained in performance appraisal and giving feedback on progress
- broad outline of how supervisor training will be given (ie training methods, when it should be given, when refresher training would be advisable, etc)
- name of person responsible for giving this training and providing checklists, etc as necessary.

Drawing up an induction policy need not be onerous; a simple one may mean that one person is responsible for most activities and that only broad outlines are needed. It is vital to gain the agreement and commitment of top management to ensure that inter-departmental rivalries or conflicting priorities do not sabotage the induction of valuable new staff.

The budgetary element is particularly important, otherwise great plans founder because nobody can decide who should pay. Giving the personnel department the budget also means that newcomers are treated consistently, each being given similar training and orientation, avoiding élites in sections where budgets are larger.

Ready for the first day

Good, effective pre-induction will mean that the first day for the newcomer will not come as a surprise.

Pre-induction checklist

1. Have they been given joining instructions?
2. Have you decided where they will sit?
3. Have you told others to expect them?
4. Have you allocated sufficient time to devote to them in the first week?
5. Have you arranged any training they may need?
6. Have you arranged any refresher induction training you may need?

3.1 Pre-induction checklist

Tick each item as it is completed:

1. ☐ Has the offer letter been sent?
2. ☐ Has acceptance been received?
3. ☐ Have joining instructions been issued? To include:

   – reporting instructions – who to, where to, what time
   – transport routes and map
   – request to bring all requisite information, eg P45, birth certificate, etc.
4. ☐ Has the welcome pack been sent?
5. ☐ Has the manager put time aside in the first week(s) to talk to the newcomer?
6. ☐ Has the manager organised work and appropriate but easy reading matter for the newcomer's first day(s)?
7. ☐ Has the last incumbent been asked to leave notes about the job?
8. ☐ Has the office space/desk/locker, etc been cleaned, prepared and equipped?
9. ☐ Have security passes, nameplate for door, business cards, computer passwords/access, cash floats, keys, etc been ordered or authorised for the newcomer?
10. ☐ Has the supervisor briefed himself or herself on the terms and conditions applicable to the newcomer and induction policy and practice?
11. ☐ Has the manager arranged any necessary refresher training for himself or herself on how to train/coach, etc?
12. ☐ Has the newcomer been booked on to an induction course and any other training programmes required? (Were any training needs suggested during their selection?)
13. ☐ Has a buddy been chosen and briefed?
14. ☐ Have the post room and switchboard been told the newcomer's name, job title, date of arrival, room number and telephone number?
15. ☐ Have other people been told when the newcomer is arriving and who they are?

3.2 Letter offering a job

On letterheaded paper

(Name)
(Address)

(Date)

Dear

Further to your recent interview and as discussed, I am pleased to offer you a post as (job title), on Grade , starting on (date), on the terms and conditions set out in this letter and on the enclosed statement of terms and conditions. This offer is subject to the receipt of satisfactory references and your passing the company's medical examination.

Employment prior to your employment under this offer will not count as part of your continuous employment with (company name) for statutory purposes.

Your starting salary will be £00,000 per annum including £0,000 London Weighting (Outer London), payable monthly in arrears by credit transfer. Subject to satisfactory efficiency and conduct, your pay will be increased annually in accordance with the attached pay scale. Your salary will be reviewed again at the end of your probationary period.

Your normal hours of work will be 00 hours per week, Monday to Friday, between (eg 9.30 am to 5.30 pm). You will be entitled to one hour unpaid meal break each day. Because of the nature of this position you may be asked to work additional hours without further pay, should this be necessary to fulfil your responsibilities.

Your appointment will be subject to a trial period of 00 months, during which time you will be expected to demonstrate your suitability for employment through your performance, attendance and conduct. During this period your employment may be terminated by one week's notice on either side. Thereafter, the periods of notice to terminate your employment are as set out in the enclosed statement of terms and conditions. The probationary period may be extended at the discretion of (company name).

Information is enclosed which outlines the factors you will need to consider when making your choice. I do very much hope that you will decide to join us.

If you would like to accept this offer, would you please confirm your acceptance of the post and conditions in writing, using the enclosed form. If you have any queries you would like to discuss, please do not hesitate to contact me, on (telephone number). If you have not accepted this offer by (date), we will assume that you do not wish to do so.

Yours sincerely,

(Name)

(Title)

Form to be enclosed with offer letter

I have read the enclosed documents:

Letter dated (date) with offer of employment as (job title)
Statement of terms and conditions of employment
Pay scale for grade
Explanatory leaflet on (eg sick pay and benefits, pension scheme, etc)
Statement of (company name)'s basic rules
Statement of (company name)'s equal opportunities policy

and would like to accept this offer of employment on the terms and conditions stated in the letter and enclosures of (date). I have retained copies of these.

I have signed the Disclosure of Information form and return it herewith.

Signed: ______________________ Date: ______________________

Name (block capitals) ______________________

Address ______________________

____

____

Daytime telephone number ______________________

3.3 Letter containing joining instructions

On letterheaded paper

(Name)
(Address)

(Date)

Dear

____ (job title)

Thank you for signing and returning your acceptance of the post named above, commencing on (date). We are very pleased that you have decided to join us and look forward to working with you.

Would you please report initially to the reception desk at (time), at:

____ (location)

____

____

____

and ask for (name). Please bring this letter with you for identification. I have enclosed a map which shows the exact location of (building name), together with the entrance you should use. The car park is also marked on the map – please let me know if you intend to drive here, and I shall issue a parking permit. On the reverse of the map are shown the public transport routes to this building.

When you arrive on the first day, would you please bring the following items with you:

- your P45 or National Insurance number
- details of the bank or building society account into which you would like your salary to be paid, including the account number, sort code, and name and address of the branch
- educational certificates (with authorised English translations)
- work permit or stamped passport
- driving licence.

The period from (time) to (time) will be spent dealing with the routine employment documentation, after which you will be taken to meet (name), your new manager. One of your new colleagues, (name) has been assigned to help you settle in during your first few days/weeks, and he/she will probably telephone you before you join to introduce himself/herself.

I have enclosed (company name)'s Welcome Pack, which I hope will make interesting reading before you join us.

I hope that you will enjoy working with us and look forward to seeing you on (date). If you have any queries, please do not hesitate to contact me on the above number.

Yours sincerely,

(Name)
(Title)

3.4 Welcome letter

On letterheaded paper

(Name)
(Address)

(Date)

Dear

Congratulations on your new appointment and welcome to (company name). As you know, I will be your manager in the Department.

I have enclosed our Welcome Pack, which I hope will help to give you a better understanding of the company and our values. The booklet gives you a brief description of some of our better-known products and services, and some export items that you may not have heard of. The pack should also give you a better idea of the working environment and the facilities we offer to our staff.

A job description and organisation charts are also enclosed so that you can put your job into context. The organisation chart for our department shows the names of the present jobholders, some of whom you met at your interview.

I hope you will find the enclosures helpful. Naturally you will learn more once you are working with us and further details will be given to you at a formal induction course. If there is anything that you would like to discuss or that you would like further information on, please telephone me, or make a note of it so that we can discuss it during your first few days.

You will find the guide useful to keep at hand during your first few months, as a reference and as somewhere to jot down further useful information.

I look forward to meeting you again soon.

Yours sincerely,

(Name)
(Title)

3.5 Checklist of Welcome Pack enclosures

1. Job description
2. Organisation chart – board and directors
3. Organisation chart – departments
4. Organisation chart – *x* department (with names)
5. Leaflet on company products and services (ideally written for the newcomer)
6. Leaflet on training opportunities, job performance and the appraisal system, discipline and grievance procedures, company equal opportunities statement, safety notices, security, holiday entitlements, etc
7. Leaflet giving brief details of sickness benefit, company pension scheme, life insurance and health care
8. Leaflet on staff benefits, including staff canteen, sports and social clubs, staff discounts on company products
9. Information on pay, how it is made up, when it is paid into the account, getting an advance on salary in the first six months, etc
10. Information for newcomers produced by the staff association or trade union
11. Brief details of assigned buddy, biography and photograph
12. Pack folder containing welcome letter from the managing director.

3.6 Notification of engagement sheet – for personnel use

EMPLOYMENT HISTORY RECORD
Recruitment source:

SURNAME | Forenames | Department | Payroll no

JOB TITLE | Starting date

ADDRESS__________ Date of birth__________
__________ Sex__________
__________ Ethnic origin__________
__________Postcode__________ Tel no__________
Nationality__________ Work permit seen: Yes/No/Not applic
Starting salary £__________ Hours of work: F/T/P/T__________
Actual pro-rata salary £__________
References taken up__________ Satisfactory/Unsatisfactory
Comments__________
Driving licence__________ Birth certificate__________
Proof of qualifications__________

P45/P46 received__________ National Insurance no__________
Bank account no__________ Payroll no__________
Bank sort code__________ Union check-off__________
Entered pension scheme__________

Probationary period: Six months/other____________________

Probationary period finishes__________ Interview date__________

Contract issued________________ Returned________________

Type of contract: Permanent/Other____________________

Annual holiday entitlement____days Entitlement this year____days

Name and address of next of kin____________________

____

____

Name of doctor________________ Tel no________________

Address____________________________________

Disabled person's reg no____________________________

Nature of disability______________________________

____

Previous occupation with group________________________

____

Retirement date________________________________

Date of leaving________________________________

Reason for leaving______________________________

____

____

Suitable for re-engagement Yes/No

Chapter 4

The First Few Days

More happens on the first days than appears on the surface. The newcomer and co-workers will test each other out, checking whether they can be trusted, whether they can work together, whether it is better to be direct or subtle. Some new employees will be cautious, watching to see what behaviour is acceptable. Others will be more active and confident.

The needs of new employees in the first days are many and varied. They need to know about:

- the environment and surroundings (in terms of layout of the area, where facilities are, travelling arrangements, etc)
- the people they will meet (colleagues, workmates, peers, bosses, subordinates, etc and some understanding of their relative positions)
- the job itself (what it entails, what the routine is, what is not included in the job, where the boundaries lie between this job and others, the limits of authority, the standards required, how the work and performance will be measured, what information is needed, etc)
- the company (what it makes or provides and how, who it employs and where, what facilities it offers, the rules it makes and who enforces them, its customers and suppliers, the security it gives, the pride it engenders, unwritten rules, etc).

There are many elements to the job that the newcomer may not be aware of:

- the challenge of the job
- availability of information and methods of communication
- frequency of contact with others
- group dynamics and current internal power struggles
- the language – jargon, acronyms and abbreviations
- who to trust and reliability of peers, subordinates and bosses
- feedback mechanisms – frequency and quality
- expectations of the group.

However, not all the needs are immediate and discretion must be used to help them build up the knowledge and divide it into manageable chunks of information, so that it can be digested and internalised, with the most important parts learned first. Although the newcomer will need to know about the company, their first concern will be about what they themselves will actually *do*.

This chapter covers the basic generic information needs and dos and don'ts for the first few days, assuming that the newcomer is beginning at work. More detailed checklists are given at the end of this chapter.

Some companies and local authorities take new staff away for up to a week for lectures and training exercises, where they are met by a top manager or executive (see Chapter 5 on the induction course). The first week spent actually at work should then follow the outline below.

Immediate needs

For induction to be successful, all parties need to believe that it will work. A positive attitude is important.

The first day should be a short one, with the new employee starting late and leaving earlier than normal. Beginning a new job is very tiring as there are so many new experiences and so much information to digest – not just details of the job and the company, but all the other drains on the memory such as trying to remember names and where everything is. The quantity of information in the first days means that retention is likely to be low, so managers and supervisors should not be surprised when they have to repeat things. Try to empathise, and remember what you felt like on the first day.

For all but the higher grades of staff, it is usual for the first day, and perhaps the first week, to be prescribed. Time is scheduled for meeting people and for giving information. However, opportunities to let newcomers use their own initiative should be increasingly sought, depending on how they appear to be coping. New employees should be actively encouraged to ask questions (how else will they find the answers they need?), and to watch, read and listen. Without encouragement newcomers may feel inhibited about asking questions, thinking it makes them look stupid. In some cultures, people avoid asking questions because they do not want their boss to lose face by having to repeat or explain, implying that they did not teach this properly the first time.

On arrival

When the newcomer arrives, it is important that reception, or whoever is to greet them, expects them. They should know where to direct them and should be welcoming. The last thing a newcomer wants is to be greeted by a blank look on the first day.

The manager should also be expecting them. There is nothing worse for the newcomer than meeting a new boss who has forgotten that they are joining that day.

If the manager or workspace is located at the other end of a maze of corridors, someone should be on hand to show the newcomer exactly where to go.

Basic information

The newcomer may first be introduced to the manager, or may go directly to the personnel department to complete the initial documentation. There is a lot of information to be gathered, and where possible this should be broken down into manageable chunks, so that the new recruit is not completely swamped. However, some details will be best collected immediately, and these include:

- the P45 and Statutory Sick Pay (SSP) forms as applicable
- National Insurance number
- bank or building society details, for payment
- checking birth certificate
- checking work permit or passport stamps, as applicable
- proof of qualifications
- checking driving licence
- checking first aid qualifications
- taking details of next of kin (in case of emergency), and name and address of doctor, etc
- checking new address and telephone number, if applicable
- taking any relevant details of pensions, etc.

The contractual details should be discussed to ensure that the newcomer understands the important clauses. People need to know the date on which they will first be paid (particularly important if the newcomer is joining at the end of a month, and will not receive payment until the end of the following month) and whether applications for advances on salary will be considered. New employees will be interested in confirming how much the basic pay is, what additional monies can be expected, when this might increase and how to check their payslip.

For employees who will be mobile, details of how to claim expenses should be given on the first morning, together with their monetary 'float' and keys to the company car, car parking permit or space number, etc, as applicable. If the newcomer has not driven the model before, check that they know where all the controls are. Where security arrangements necessitate passcards, etc, these should be issued.

There should be some brief discussion about the new items of written information given, with the opportunity to discuss them in detail later should the need arise. Brief reasons *why* the policies and practices have been agreed will help them to remember and understand them and respect the organisation. This will take time but is important. New recruits will hardly be encouraged if they are given a huge mound of unsorted and unexplained paperwork, with the words, 'I've been told to give you these', before the speaker shuffles off to 'get on with something more important'.

New information can include:

- employee handbook
- details of company policies, such as equal opportunities, rules for dealing with the public, safety, etc
- discipline and grievance procedure, and what to do and who to talk to if there are problems or complaints
- rules on conduct, dress, house style, etc, where these have not been given before
- company car documentation
- company newsletter and/or annual report.

Some of the information need not be given to the newcomer on the first day, but can be dealt with on a formal induction course, eg details of company policies, etc.

Newcomers should be informed of any information held on them on computer databases, and that they will have the opportunity to check it. If they are to be permitted access to paper files, this should also be explained.

Basic information needs also cover fire and first aid procedures and any particular safety measures for the areas in which they will be working. Protective clothing and/or uniforms or image clothing should be issued as appropriate.

One further useful piece of paper is a large scale map of the local area, showing the position of banks, post offices, dry cleaners, shoemenders, major stores, etc.

The initial discussion

Once the new employee and the personnel department have completed all the paperwork, it will be time to meet the new manager (again). The initial chat should cover mutual expectations and give them an idea of what to expect over the first day and the first week. Initial discussions are important; the manager has control over the information given and must check understanding. In many cases newcomers will not recognise information which is relevant to them; they may think that they understand while maintaining their perceptions of how things are done from their past job.

Building the relationship

The manager should begin by establishing rapport, taking the first steps to build a relationship based on mutual respect. Taking an interest in how the newcomer found the travelling and what their first impressions were will help to create a good working relationship. The newcomer should be treated like a child only in that you attempt to establish early bonding! Show that you are devoting time to them and spending money on them – that they matter. Show that they are a valuable part of the organisation by emphasising the essential role of the individual in the company (but without intimidating them).

It is a good idea to give the newcomer a notebook early on (or there may be space in the Welcome Pack or induction booklet) so that they can make notes. Suggest that they write memory-joggers as appropriate. It is useful to set the scene at the beginning, telling them that you expect them to tell you if they are having problems. Managers should naturally try to assess this, but they are not clairvoyant. Newcomers should be encouraged to ask questions to clarify any areas they are not sure of and to ask for help when they need it. It may be useful to tell them what time you are setting aside for them in the first week, so that they can ask questions then. This will help to allay their anxieties and take the pressure off.

Anxieties are likely to include:

- worry that they can't do the job
- worry that they will not remember all the names (of people, places and things)
- worry that they will get lost
- a feeling of being overwhelmed and tired.

Worries vary. Young people may worry about fitting in, making friends, making mistakes and whether the boss will be understanding. Senior managers may be more concerned about getting the information they need to make good decisions, whether subordinates can be trusted, whether they can beat the competition, earn credibility and profit, and create a good organisational climate. Women and people from ethnic minorities may worry about being harassed or not taken seriously.

Particularly if they are excited by the new job, the feeling of tiredness may come as a surprise to the newcomer, who may not realise how stressful a new job can be and how wearing it is to be given such a large amount of new information.

Discussion of the organisation chart can help to show the newcomer where they fit in, and will tie in with what they need to know about their own level of authority relative to others, and the limits of their responsibility. In public organisations, the relationship between elected members and the officers may be explored. The manager should recap on the general activities of the organisation.

The supervisor or manager should talk through the job description or checklist of work and tell the newcomer about the work to be tackled immediately. The manager must make it clear which is more important – speed or accuracy. Some jobs must be done quickly at the expense of quality, others must be completed meticulously even if it takes a long time.

The manager should talk about standards, say how the new employee's performance will be assessed, and discuss the frequency of progress meetings, etc. The importance of the probationary period should be re-emphasised, so that the new employee is encouraged and the standards are clear. Probation is about being fair: the newcomer must be in no doubt that if their performance does not match the expected level, their employment will not be continued. It should also be clear that guidance will be given, and that the manager will help them to attain the required standards, through training or coaching.

Meaningful work

New employees need to be given appropriate and meaningful work on the first day, so that they feel they are gainfully employed and are beginning to achieve something. They should be busy rather than bored, but not merely be left to read through company material, which they are unlikely to take in fully anyway. Most newcomers want to do something useful, and will feel vaguely guilty if they are just reading while colleagues are seen beavering away. Giving a real job also shows trust and allows the individual to start taking control of their own time.

The tasks set should not be mundane (although there may be some of those too!). The employee should begin their own job and should *not* have to take on all the department's worst jobs or the responsibilities of the office junior for the first few days until people have got used to them. However, they should not be set too much of a challenge initially – this can build up gradually as they progress. Supervision may be needed but should not be too obvious. If their task is written, it may be useful to give examples of other pieces of work as a model.

Avoid giving the new recruit reading to do simply because you are not sure what else they can do. The first tasks may be difficult as everything is so new and the newcomer may be uncertain of their capabilities, but having real work to do will take the focus away from the difficulties of the newness. The manager must also avoid dumping a heavy workload on the newcomer at first. The new employee may be especially prone to this if the organisation is or has been understaffed. Seeing the newcomer, the group's sighs of relief are almost palpable and the recruit takes on a rapidly growing in-tray.

The manager should be available to answer questions, or assign someone else who is responsible to help the newcomer. The new employee may be asked to save up questions which do not need immediate answers, so that others can get on with their work uninterrupted while the newcomer begins the first tasks. It is also helpful if the last jobholder has left notes about the job, showing peak and slacker periods, what happens in a typical day, and tips on how to perform various duties. Checklists and project planning wall charts can also help. If the last incumbent was promoted or transferred and is still on hand to answer questions, so much the better.

The manager may also need to address other problems, such as whether (and if so, how) to tell the newcomer that someone else in the department applied for the post. If one of the newcomer's subordinates was not considered promotable just yet, the newcomer will have to find a way of building the relationship and ensuring that the individual continues to make a contribution and develop in their job. This is a tricky area, and how it is handled will depend on the positions and personalities involved.

Normal working hours should also be discussed, so that the new employee knows when to arrive and depart, and there should be some discussion of informal codes and rules, such as the acceptability of personal telephone calls, etc. These grey areas often leave newcomers feeling uneasy, and are best tackled directly and early on. Office politics may also be addressed, but beware of passing on prejudices.

The manager or supervisor should show the new employee their desk, locker or work area, etc, ensuring that adequate tools, equipment or stationery, etc are available. It is common practice to give the newcomer the oldest and poorest equipment – avoid this if possible. If they are likely to require further supplies, they should be told where these are and how to obtain them. They should be issued with other sundries as appropriate:

- locker keys
- uniforms or image clothing
- protective clothing
- clock card or key
- operating or safety manuals for particular equipment.

Although they may not undertake it personally, it is the manager's responsibility to ensure that the newcomer knows where the toilets are, where coats and belongings can be left and where to obtain lunch, coffee, tea or cold drinks, etc.

It is a good idea to ensure that the newcomer will have company for lunch or meal breaks each day in the first week, as being left alone in a strange place can make them feel stranded. However, they will have other needs too, such as popping out to the bank, or doing routine shopping, so should not necessarily be expected to 'join the crowd' for lunch each day.

The manager should check regularly that everything is all right during the first few days. Friendly faces and kindness are important. New employees who are ignored may withdraw physically and/or mentally and often develop a less positive attitude to the work and the company.

Meeting the team

The immediate manager is normally the person who will introduce the newcomer to other workmates and colleagues. The manager cannot make friends for them but can mention common interests. Introductions should be quite short; few people know quite what to say after the initial, 'Hello, where did you work before, how long have you been here?' lines, particularly with the manager looking on. Often the newcomer may be ignored as the person who was being introduced remembers a work matter on which they want to consult the manager.

Although it may be useful to give a brief tour of the work area, the 'handshake tour' is rarely effective, as the newcomer sees an ever-increasing sea of faces, and it becomes harder and harder to remember the matching names. It will be more useful to give a plan of the area, and to meet a couple of new people at a time, spread over the first fortnight or so.

Where the newcomer will have a lot of contacts, and introductory meetings have already been set up, they should be told of this. It is appropriate in some situations for them to be given the telephone numbers of the first people to talk to, so that the newcomer can arrange their own introductory meetings. A little guidance on who is most approachable will be well received, as long as this is not accompanied by age-old prejudices and all the local gossip. Newcomers should be allowed to make up their own minds, while receiving warning of any obvious difficulty.

If the newcomer is likely to be working mainly alone or with only one other, introductions to other people are even more important, as there is no ready-made team for them to get to know first. It is particularly important that they should not be left in an isolated office and expected to get to know people entirely through their own initiative.

Diary dates should be given for department-wide commitments, such as team meetings/briefings or monthly meetings between sales and customer service sections, etc and for their formal induction course and any staff association or union meetings.

If the new person is likely to be approached by union representatives or shop stewards, they should be told. If there is a choice of unions, this should also be explained.

Care should be taken to ensure that newcomers are not excluded from social activities during the initial period – a common, if unintended error.

Office grapevine

The 'grapevine' is often a very effective and speedy means of communication, and you should not be in any doubt that the newcomer will soon be included.

The latest rumours and gossip can be unsettling for newcomers, particularly if they concern such things as impending redundancies or relocation, where the new recruit is bound to feel that their job is under threat because they are the newest, or that an office move is imminent. To lessen the impact of any rumours relating to the job, a warning about what they are likely to hear, whether it is true or not, and the management's 'official' line can be given.

It is often easy for a newcomer to 'put his foot in it' by making a comment about somebody without knowing of their relationship to the person they are talking to. Even if this comment is a positive one, they may feel uncomfortable afterwards and will appreciate being told who is married to whom, or going out with whom, etc. Naturally, as mentioned above, this should be handled with discretion and subtlety and not given out as the latest gossip!

The 'buddy'

Many organisations assign a 'buddy', 'sponsor' or 'starter's friend' to the newcomer. This person should show them the ropes and be on hand to answer questions informally as they arise. Buddying is a temporary arrangement to help the newcomer in the early days.

The buddy should preferably be of around the same age and grade as the newcomer, so that they are likely to have some things in common. It helps if the buddy is relatively new to the organisation, because they will remember all the initial queries and uncertainties. Alternatively, assigning the buddy role to another team member may be a useful way of giving responsibility. The buddy should be accepted by the work group so that they can help the new person to gain acceptance. The buddy should be willing to help the newcomer rather than be an unwilling or disinterested nominee.

The buddy may make contact with the newcomer before their arrival, and may be the person who takes them to lunch during the first week. They can show them where things are, and perform some of the introductions. The buddy can give practical tips and needs to be interruptable. Consequently their output during this initial period should not be expected to be high. If their earnings are normally related to output, a minimum should be guaranteed to compensate.

The buddy performs a valuable function in taking some of the pressure off the manager or supervisor, who is unlikely to be able to spend all day with the newcomer. The buddy may also be involved in giving on-the-job tuition to the newcomer, and can show how to operate basic equipment such as photocopiers, telephones and faxes and what to do with the post. They may also demonstrate how to log on to computers, generate passwords and use basic programs, etc. The buddy should help them to decode procedural manuals so that they understand how to do things, and make sense of the budgets, etc. They may also be involved in giving feedback on performance so that the newcomer knows how they are doing.

It will be useful if the buddy introduces the newcomer to the group norms or unwritten rules – on how they work, for instance:

(a) We only take breaks at prescribed times; or
(b) We come and go as we please.

(a) We voice disagreements and sometimes have heated arguments; or
(b) We are polite and cool in dissent and try not to upset colleagues.

(a) We always double-check information with the boss before it passes to other departments; or
(b) We are trusted to provide accurate information to others and this is rarely checked.

(a) We help each other to get the work done, all 'mucking in'; or
(b) We all do our own bit but do not get involved in the work of others.

This kind of information is useful, but remember that you will need to tell the buddy what you expect them to do rather than leaving it all to their own judgement.

First day round-up

At the end of the first day (which should be earlier than usual for the new recruit), the manager should review the information given and received and reiterate the job requirements.

The manager should give encouragement and reassurance, eg, 'I am very pleased with the way in which you appear to have grasped things today. I'm sure that you'll settle in quickly and soon be able to undertake your job competently.' It is important to express confidence in the new person, and also to avoid 'war stories' such as, 'Ha! You thought this was busy, did you? Well, just wait till you see it at the end of the month!' – hardly an encouragement and you may worry them considerably.

The second day

The second day should start where the first day left off, with an overview of the job. The manager should begin by repeating the main points given on the first day, answering any questions and providing a little more information.

In the first weeks

There is no short cut to spending time with new employees, which pays dividends later. Make sure that even if they work mainly alone, they are not isolated during the initial period.

It is advisable to have regular progress meetings in the short term, perhaps daily in the first week, then weekly and monthly as dictated by the support and guidance they require. This is particularly important for those in jobs which take them away from their base a lot, and for homeworkers.

If the manager is overcritical initially, or continues to be, the newcomer's confidence can be undermined or will never develop. Eventually they may become depressed and leave. (See also Chapter 7 on feedback.)

It will be useful for the new starter to meet the manager's manager (their 'grandparent' boss) early on, so that they see them as approachable and not as strange and distant beings to be feared or worried about. Meeting this person will help them to adjust and fit in, and to feel valued.

Where the newcomer spends some time in each department, they should be left with the people there so that areas of responsibility can be outlined without the manager standing by and inhibiting the staff.

In some organisations, and for some grades of staff, a mentor will be assigned to the newcomer. This person is usually several rungs up the hierarchical ladder and can give advice about their career and potential. (See Chapter 7 for more detail.)

Information to be covered in the first few weeks includes:

- background
- organisation chart, and limits of authority
- geographical layout
- policies, and why they exist
- rules, regulations and procedures
- health and safety
- communications
- employee benefits and rights
- responsibilities of the job.

Some of these will be covered by the supervisor at the workplace, others will be dealt with during a formal induction course (see the next chapter). In small companies, where formal courses may not be appropriate, the information will nearly all be conveyed by the immediate superior.

Checklist for the first days

1. Have you greeted the new employee?
2. Has the basic employment documentation been completed?
3. Have you shown them the layout, including their work area and toilets, cloakrooms and canteens, etc?
4. Have you discussed basic requirements such as hours of work and attendance?
5. Have you talked them through the job description, given them meaningful work and encouraged them to ask questions?
6. Have you introduced them to their co-workers?
7. Have you assigned a buddy and told them what to do?
8. Have you given the newcomer encouragement and reassurance?
9. Have you recapped on information already given?

4.1 Induction notes for supervisors

Importance of induction

Induction is the process of settling into a new job. The induction programme helps newcomers to settle in faster because information is provided in a cohesive and structured manner. This will help them to feel involved and therefore settle in more quickly, becoming more productive earlier.

Induction is important:

- Economic factors demand that staff know how to do their jobs effectively and as quickly as possible. Well-trained staff are cost-effective.
- Natural justice dictates that if we set high standards, we should equip staff to achieve them. (No one comes to the job fully equipped, no matter how experienced they are, or what level of job or salary they have.)
- Good induction prevents an exodus of disillusioned staff and increased staff turnover. This keeps company costs down and staff morale higher (because frequently covering vacant jobs is draining on morale).

Everybody will feel anxious (as well as excited) about a new job. Anxieties arise as much from their not being part of an established work group or knowing what behaviour is expected, as from ignorance of company rules and the newness of the working environment.

A newcomer who remains anxious will not learn the job easily. This may lead to a feeling of inadequacy and frustration, which may in turn lead to dissatisfaction with the company and the job.

The success of the induction programme depends largely on delivering the right information at the right time in the right way. It is neither practical nor desirable to prescribe what should happen to the newcomer for each hour of each day. There must be flexibility to allow for the needs of the company and the individual. It is your job to ascertain the individual needs and match these to company needs so that training can be adapted appropriately.

The newcomer needs to know about the job, the company, the people, the working environment, and the rules and regulations.

What to include in the induction programme

Use your checklist and examine the induction course programme so that you can give information appropriately, dovetailing what you tell the newcomer with what they will learn on the formal course. It will help if you have undergone refresher training in how to train and coach staff.

How to train

Remember the basics – see if you can find out how the newcomer learns best (what their preferred learning style is) and break the training up into manageable chunks. If the newcomer seems to have reached a plateau and is not progressing or seems tired, vary the task so that they can try something else, returning to the other when they feel fresher.

Don't expect too much of them – people learn at different paces. Give praise and constructive criticism (less of the latter if possible):

- specifically, with examples
- at the time
- clearly.

Make sure that it is something they can change (not an aspect of personality, but focusing on their behaviour). Say why it pleased or displeased you (ie you are subjective, it is not an absolute truth).

Show and say that you are confident they will learn the task/get the hang of the problem, etc. Give examples of the kinds of problem that others have and the usual learning time, so that they avoid the obvious pitfalls and don't try to attempt too much at first.

Vary the instructions or description of how to do something if they don't appear to respond or understand; try putting the same thing another way.

Plan how you will give the information, both about rules, etc and for job training. Think about how it was explained to you – did that work well? What else did you want to know? Which other methods do you know that worked well for other people?

If you have difficulties, ask the training department – they are there to help you.

Be available

Be available to the newcomer to answer questions, provide information and maintain social contact. Check progress and how they feel about it regularly.

Remember to brief the buddy, and be available to answer their questions too.

4.2 Supervisor's induction checklist

All items should have been explained to the employee by the end of their fourth week. Each item should be initialled and dated as it is completed.

Responsibility: ______________________________ (supervisor's name)

New employee: ______________________________ (name)

Job title: ____________________ Start date: ____________________

Date of supervisor's refresher training: ______________________________

THE FIRST DAY

Environment

Where to hang coat
Location of toilets and rest rooms
Arrangements for lunch and refreshments
Hours of work – arrival and leaving times, flexitime or clocking on procedures, lateness and punctuality
Emergency evacuation procedure, extinguishers, alarm buttons, exits and assembly points
Exits and entrances
Location of car park
Give map of local area – internal, showing departments; external showing major landmarks, banks, etc
Location of personal work area
Safety/security of personal belongings

About the job

Explain duties and responsibilities of job, expectations, to whom to refer problems
Discuss objectives, work of department
Introduction to 2–3 colleagues, and buddy
Safety/security of office equipment and records
No smoking/eating areas, unauthorised areas/zones
Right of search
Other (list):

THE FIRST WEEKS

The supervisor should ensure that as many as possible of the following points are covered in the first week. The list is not exhaustive or meant to be covered in sequence.

Terms and conditions

Absences from work – notification procedure, procedure for sickness at work
Holidays – how to book, when they can be taken, carrying over unused holidays, check any holidays already booked
Salary – when, how paid, deductions, where to raise queries
Security of employment, probationary period, notice period
Pensions/superannuation, share schemes, profit sharing, bonus, etc
Staff discounts
Explain social/recreational facilities
Appearance and behaviour
Personal problems – who to see

Health, safety and security

Accidents at work – prevention, reporting, first aid
Accident prevention – clear corridors, housekeeping, not blocking exits, correct lifting procedures
Hazardous substances/processes
Protective clothing and its cleaning
Alcohol and operation of equipment
No electrical equipment/tools operated until training received
Personal hygiene and smoking policy/arrangements
Organise security pass

Office services and miscellaneous

Explanation of typing/reprographic facilities
Telephone system and post arrangements
Private use of telephones
Expenses – what can be claimed, when, how
Travelling arrangements
Use of computers – passwords, danger of viruses, software to be used

Legal and communications

Issue company handbook
Discuss contract of employment
Legal requirements relevant to duties and working environment
Confidentiality of work
Location of notice boards, internal communications/newspaper
Staff association/trade union details

Training and promotion

Check date of induction course
Training – release time, what paid training is available, who to ask for further information
Promotion, career prospects

Company handbook

Discussion of:
Discipline/grievance
Appraisal and performance review
Equal opportunities
Health and safety policy and practices
Company philosophy and public relations
Company structure, names of top people
Main products/services
Future developments and expansion
The place of the company within the industry
Numbers employed
Locations of company buildings.

4.3 Sample timetable for office worker's first and second days

THE FIRST DAY

Time	*Activity*	*People involved*
10.30	Employee arrives	
	Greeting by reception and personnel	reception personnel
10.45	Paperwork	personnel
	Collect P45 and other documentation	
	Give company information pack	
	Provide map of local area and buildings	
	Introduce safety policy and requirements	
11.45	Take newcomer to meet new manager	personnel
11.55	Initial chat with new manager	immediate
	Establish rapport – discuss weather!	manager
	Discuss the hierarchy chart	
	Show them their desk (give them coffee)	
	Introduce buddy	
12.30	Buddy shows them fire exits, etc	buddy
	Buddy takes them to lunch	
13.30	Newcomer goes back to manager	manager
	Discussion of:	
	the main points about the job	
	how work will be monitored	
	appraisal and probationary period	
	hours of work, etc	
	Give task they can begin work on	manager
	Give further reading matter	
14.15	Introductions to immediate colleagues	manager
	(2 or 3)	co-workers
14.30	Leave them to get on with first tasks	newcomer
16.30	Conduct discussion and first day round-up	manager
16.45	Send newcomer home	manager

THE SECOND DAY

Time	*Activity*	*People involved*
09.00	New employee arrives	newcomer
09.15	Discussion with manager: more about the job feedback on task Manager tells newcomer when available to answer questions about the work, etc	manager
09.30	Newcomer continues meaningful work	newcomer
10.30	Coffee break and introduction to a few other new colleagues	manager
10.45	Newcomer continues meaningful work	newcomer
12.30	Ask newcomer to join group for lunch	manager
13.30	Discussion with buddy on aspects of the job	buddy
14.00	More work and/or reading company information	newcomer
15.30	Tea with colleagues	
15.45	Back to previous tasks	newcomer
16.45	Second day round-up – discussion with manager	manager
17.00	Finish work	

4.4 Checklists for induction topics

The following checklists cover most of the main items you might have to tell new staff about. This list cannot be exhaustive but gives examples of the main areas, and should be sufficient to remind you of other related details that apply in your place of work.

To enable you to use discrete sections, you will find that a few items are listed more than once as they are applicable in various sections.

Checklist A: Rules and contractual details

1. Hours of work, etc

Attendance, punctuality, lateness, time cards, clocking in and clock cards

Shift arrangements, shift rotas and pay

Overtime, weekend working

On call allowances, being called up or called out, vehicles to be used for call-outs, maximum time to respond, use of pagers

Rules on breaks, eg lunch, tea or coffee breaks, etc

2. Housekeeping, security and equipment

Security arrangements – site security, passcards, keys, petty cash and floats, transport of cash, last out procedures (eg closing windows at night, turning off machines and electrical switches, etc), emergency phone numbers, storage and security of personal belongings, compensation for damage to personal property, lost property, theft and fraud (eg procedures for dealing with, disciplinary offences, etc), right of search

Confidentiality, commercial and official secrets, intellectual property rights, disclosure of information, rules on data protection, etc, computer passwords, avoidance of computer viruses

Maintenance and transportation of company property and equipment, use of fork-lift trucks and transporters, etc, issue of log books and manuals and how to use them

Speed limits on site, pedestrian areas, traffic barriers, taking deliveries, etc

Energy conservation – use of power and lighting

Insurance – company insurance, public liability insurance, personal cover, travel insurance, what is not covered

3. Health and safety, fire and first aid

Health and safety regulations, personal responsibility, etc, need for good housekeeping and avoiding risks, keeping passages clear, tidiness

Safety procedures and health risks – dangerous substances and processes, obvious hazards, smoking regulations, non-smoking areas, danger of eating and food contamination, danger of loose clothing and hair, dangers of 'horse-play' and jokes

First aid – first aiders (who and where they are), first aid boxes and their locations and contents (and barrier creams for dermatitis, eye baths, etc), what to do if you feel unwell at work, first aid and treatment rooms, accidents outside normal hours, occupational health service

Protective clothing and footwear, styles, sizes and cost (if the employee pays), laundry, replacement

Fire procedures – fire instructions, fire notices, drills, location and use of alarms, extinguishers and exits, reporting, evacuation, use of lifts and stairs, assembly points, fire wardens, keeping passages and exits clear, causes and prevention of fire

Bomb alerts – reporting, action to be taken if bomb suspected, evacuation, suspicious parcels or packages

4. Office procedures and operation of equipment

Filing systems, how to order stationery and equipment, how to get typing or photocopying done, secretarial services, reception and procedures for greeting visitors, mail handling, mail in-trays or boxes and out-trays, etc, ordering couriers and arranging deliveries, desk or locker keys

Photocopiers – training in normal operation, unjamming, calling engineers, paper to be used, use of photocopier-safe acetates only

Telephones, etc – how to answer the telephone, internal/external calls, how to transfer calls, rotas for covering phones, phone books and use of directory enquiries, rules on long distance, international and personal calls, calling during cheap rate if possible, use of answerphones

Use of faxes, telex, etc, use of PA systems and radio pagers, etc

Computers – manuals, training on programmes, passwords and security, data protection, who can solve problems, engineers and help desks, avoiding viruses

Other equipment – training in its use, safety rules, user manuals, protective clothing and its laundry or replacement

5. Salary, wages and payments

Starting salary, date of payment, method of payment, explanation of pay statement, remuneration, compensation and benefits policies

Basic salary and when it increases, allowances, overtime payments, bonuses and incentive schemes (when and how much, targets, etc), advances on salary, maternity/paternity pay, long service awards

Deductions (income tax, National Insurance, etc), docking of salary, repayment of loans, deduction of union membership fees

Expenses – how to claim, limits on expenses, authorising signatory for expenses, what expenses can be claimed (eg travel expenses, not equipment, etc), floats

Payments for membership of professional associations

6. Employee benefits

Holidays – public holidays, arrangements for Christmas and New Year, when the holiday year begins, carrying over holiday, relationship to length of service, when holidays can be taken, when time off can't be taken, notification procedure, extended holidays, payments in lieu of holidays

Absence other than holidays – maternity/paternity leave, bereavement leave, compensatory leave, jury service, unpaid leave, time off in lieu, doctor's appointments, flexitime arrangements, time off for company competitions, etc, time off for study and examinations

Sickness – sick leave, reporting of sickness (when, who to, etc), self-certification form, when doctor's certificate is needed, medical statements, accrual of sick leave, sickness payments, Statutory Sick Pay, sick rooms, what to do if you feel unwell at work

Health – requirements for medicals, health and accident insurance, private health care scheme and arrangements, occupational health service, over 40s or well-woman screening, etc, sports and social facilities, sports teams and fitness classes, etc, welfare arrangements and who to see about problems

Life insurance and pension arrangements – employee's and employer's contributions, retirement age, how much pension is paid, contracted out or in

Profit sharing, savings schemes, share ownership schemes, long service awards

Loan schemes, educational assistance and payments, company transport, discounts on company goods

Luncheon vouchers, staff canteen, restaurants (eg opening times, menus, vegetarian or special diets, etc), vending machines

7. Company cars
Overall policy, whether contractual or not, tax and any other contributions to be made, insurance (including who is and who is not allowed to drive the car, taking the car abroad, etc), choice of car, when cars are changed, permitted extras, permitted use of other transport, use of company car by other employees

Keys, log book and handbooks, mileage rates, keeping the car clean and roadworthy, repairs and maintenance, use of hire cars during repair time, provision of maps

Car parking, car parking fines, driving offences and endorsements/points

8. Company Policies
Written statement of terms

Notice periods, holidays and payments under notice, probationary periods, grievance and appeals procedures

Job evaluation and grading, how jobs can be reassessed, why their job is graded the way it is

Discipline and dismissal – misconduct and gross misconduct, suspension, disciplinary proceedings, onus of proof, actual offences (eg theft, drunkenness, gambling, insubordination, endangering others, breaches of safety rules, etc), poor performance

Equal opportunities policies – what the policy includes, dealing with harassment and other offences, equal opportunities training, arrangements for religious observances

Other policies – alcohol, smoking, company romances, dress code and appearance, mode of address (eg Mr Smith to the Managing Director, or call him John)

9. Miscellaneous
Travel on company business – travel insurance, booking tickets, first or second class, public or private transport, air travel versus train, etc, health regulations for overseas visits, claiming overtime for travelling, use of own transport (including insurance details, carriage of company goods/materials, etc)

Maps – locations of other departments or buildings, locations of useful local amenities (banks, post offices, dry cleaners, sandwich bars, pubs, etc), public transport to and from the company, car parking

Employee entrances to buildings and sites, use of staff or rest rooms, cloakroom and toilet facilities

Chaplaincy, library, quality awards

Office norms on coffee pool, birthdays, get well cards, office leaving collections

---

Checklist B: Company information

1. About the organisation
Values and mission statement, aspirations and vision of the future, commitment to quality, business ethics

Organisation development and history, parent company and/or subsidiaries, manufacturing processes and procedures

Customers and suppliers, products and services, markets (home and international), main competitors, customer service commitment

Company structure (branches and departments), number of employees, their functional areas and locations

2. Communications
Information boards and notices, annual report, company journal or newspaper, internal job advertisements, staff handbook, company brochures

Team briefings, information cascades, quality circles, suggestion schemes, quality awards

Procedures and rules for meetings

Staff associations, unions (including constituencies, check-off arrangements, level of recognition, nationally or locally negotiated agreements, etc), other consultation arrangements, how to use/become an employee representative

Communications manuals, sales literature, house style for publications, internal telephone directories or contact lists

3. Miscellaneous
Organisation chart(s) – with names and/or photos of incumbents

Glossary of company jargon and acronyms

Checklist C: Performance of the job

1. Job description
Job description and explanation of the job, peaks and troughs of work, requirements for overtime, potential difficulties, supervision given, supervision to be given to others, relationships between this job and the department and between the department and the rest of the company

Limits of authority – theirs, their boss's and their subordinates'

2. Appraisal, standards and objectives
Appraisal – how the individual will be judged, attitudes and performance, probationary period

Standards – job performance (eg quality, wastage rates, efficiency, etc), dress codes for customer-facing staff and others, quality control

Objectives and goals – discussion of what is expected, management by objectives, goal setting, targets

Discussion of the future – what to expect in terms of promotion, wider job experience, transfers, personal development

3. Training
Training – training requirements and how those will be fulfilled, content and duration of training, training plans, study time, payment for courses, company training scheme, induction training, location of training, recording training progress

Chapter 5

Elements of a Successful Induction Course

This chapter gives some pointers on what to put in a successful induction course. Naturally, you will need to tailor this to your own organisation, but it covers standard information as well as a few ideas for running the programme a little differently. This chapter also briefly covers learning styles and memory, training aids and formats, for those of you who may never have designed a course before.

Designing the induction programme

The induction period should be linked to the length of time it takes to become effective in the job and to learn and internalise the new activities. If the job usually takes three months to learn properly, the induction programme (the planned off-the-job learning plus the formal induction course) can cover this period. If the job takes much longer to learn, it is likely to be more complex and require a greater degree of judgement, thereby necessitating a greater intake of information over a longer period.

When designing an induction programme, you will need to consider whether to hold a common induction course as part of this, and if so when, what to include in it, and which elements are best learned on the job. Look at which parts are crucial and need to be understood quickly and which can wait. Formal induction courses away from work are not necessarily needed in small companies, but the same kind of information needs to be presented.

Justifying the need for a formal induction course

There are many doubting Thomases and objectors to the principles, costs and time that induction courses involve. Induction courses are not panaceas, and must be well designed and tailored. Specific objections to courses can and should be answered. Common objections to induction courses, together with replies to them, include:

> 'Some can cope without induction training, can't they all?' 'It's élitist, we didn't get all this and it didn't do us any harm.'

Some people cope without induction training but research has shown that in general people become effective more quickly after proper induction. It is not élitist as it should be common, rather than given to the 'chosen few'.

'The course bears no relevance to what they will actually *do*.' 'It takes them away from doing/learning the job.'

If properly designed, the course will be relevant to what people do, because it will help them put it into context and understand how and why the company works the way it does. Time away from the job is usually minimal, and will help their learning.

'If they have already been around for a while, they will have discovered what they need to know, so the course is not relevant.'

There are usually things that people have not discovered, or that they do not discover until too late. There are often gaps in knowledge and things that they don't know they don't know about! Many people wish that they had been given information earlier.

'It is too expensive, both in terms of time and money.'

The induction course does not have to be an expensive affair, and is cost-effective as it helps people to become effective more quickly. Arranging the information into the form of a course means that personnel can check that new starters are getting the information and guidance that they need, in a consistent format. Misconceptions can be sorted out and gaps filled.

'It does not stop people leaving.'

It does not stop everyone leaving, but research shows that after proper induction, fewer people leave quickly.

'It is only relevant for white collar staff.'

Other workers also need to understand where they fit in the organisation. Most induction courses include sections on understanding the terms and conditions of the job, and the organisation's rules – everyone needs to know those. Where company philosophies such as a focus on customer care are covered, it is crucial to begin early with maintenance or engineering staff and junior clerical staff, as they are often the ones talking to or meeting customers.

'There is too much information for them to remember.'

There is a mass of information to be learned (see checklists)! Structuring the content will help faster absorption of the main elements. The organisation can choose the pace of learning so that the important points are covered first.

'The atmosphere is too much like being back at school.'

It does not have to be. A well-designed course will enable everyone to benefit as it uses a number of different teaching methods and takes account of different learning styles. (Supporters of this type of criticism may also find that schools have changed, of course!) Formal induction courses are in danger of becoming bureaucratic and institutionalised; constant and persistent re-evaluation should help to prevent this, as does the inclusion of self-managed learning techniques.

The 'guest speaker' does not see any direct benefit from talking to the newcomers.

This needs persuasion! One hopes that the speaker will in time realise that the individuals in their department have settled in and become effective more quickly after doing the induction course.

'There is too much incongruence between what the newcomers are told and what they see.'

This is usually a problem of culture, coupled with the fact that rules are not enforced. The problem of the differences between the company's image of itself and what the individuals perceive may need to be tackled first. Course designers should do their best to ensure that there is congruence between what people are told and what actually happens, or the newcomers may become disillusioned. If the course is highly structured and organised, but the workplace is not, this can give an unrealistic impression and inflated expectations.

Courses also give individuals opportunities to meet other new starters. Junior staff may be more open with their new peers than with supervisors and can ask questions in this forum. Sometimes they do not initially feel confident with the 'old hands' and may not be able to question them about company values or other ideals.

Considerations in course design

Having convinced the doubters at least to try it, you need to formulate the course. When designing the formal course the following considerations should be made:

Who should be consulted? The line manager, personnel, training, and safety staff and trade unions need to be consulted about the content of the programme, what is included and what left out, and how the information should be put across, ie finance people will want to influence how the financial material is explained.

should get induction? What grades of people, and should grades be mixed? What kind of people need the course?

should deliver the induction course?

should check that everything has been covered? (It is usually personnel in liaison with the supervisor, who know what is covered on the formal course, and check what on-the-job training is given.)

What needs to be covered?

are priority areas?

written information should be given?

special needs are there? (See also Chapter 6.)

will be the roles of the supervisors, personnel and training staff, etc?

When should the induction course be given? The longer they have been there, the more difficult it may be for the inductees to get time away from work.

What hours, times, days of the week? The needs of part-time workers and shiftworkers are often forgotten.

Where should the training be held? Large companies will have specially designed training facilities, others may have to negotiate space or use hotels, etc.

How should the course be structured? For example, should it be two full days or a modular approach?

should information be given? What teaching methods, visual aids, etc? Can self-managed learning be used? Are different learning styles catered for?

can the course content be linked with and related to the work?

long should the induction course be? Over what time-scales?

A formal induction policy (see the previous chapter) can cover many of these aspects.

Course content

Course objectives and content should be decided first, then prioritised by consultation with all the relevant people. (Examples of induction course programmes are given on pages 93–97.)

What is included in the formal induction course is influenced by when this is held, to avoid repetition and to fill any gaps. Consider the implications of giving training earlier or later. If labour turnover is high, people may leave before receiving induction training. If it is low, individuals may have to wait until there are enough new recruits to run an induction training course. The duration will also influence the material you will be able to cover.

Depending upon the inductees, the course need not be completely standard. A large company will contain several different sub-cultures and the course can be tailored to the different approaches of different departments. Alternatively, if the course is mixed, core values can be covered, with the departmental interpretation and emphasis picked up later by the supervisor.

It is common practice to give all the introductory and common information to people in a group session, rather than individually, and at the minimum level needed to help them work satisfactorily. This can then be augmented by the supervisor later. However, even if there are large numbers of recruits they must be given some personal attention – not everything can be covered on a course. Also, different grades may have different payments systems and course groups can be split so that they each learn about their own.

The checklists on pages 66–71 and 93 give some ideas and fuller lists of items for inclusion on an induction course. Areas that could be covered include:

- Layout of the building(s) (if not already covered)
- Contractual details and explanation of conditions of employment
- Explanation of the job, quality, quantity and standards required and how performance will be measured
- Company background – history, products, image, etc
- Company rules, procedures and values
- Safety, first aid and fire procedures, etc
- Security arrangements and housekeeping
- Office procedures and operation of equipment, etc (if not already covered)
- Employee benefits and facilities
- Education, training and promotion opportunities
- Internal communications and where to look for further information.

Some of these will be covered at the workplace by the supervisor. Discussion with supervisors will help those responsible for formulating the courses to decide on areas not covered and how these should be dealt with on the induction course. It helps the integration of the newcomers if the line managers take part in the induction course.

Safety is an important topic for inclusion on the induction course, even if it has been covered to some extent by the supervisor. Research has shown that the frequency of accidents decreases with length of experience, and it is the employer's legal responsibility to give employees a healthy, safe place to work and to help them maintain this. Just as good personnel managers want to avoid excessive staff turnover, an accident-free environment must also be ensured. The dangers are all too obvious; unsafe working practices are bad for everyone – bad for the company and its image, bad for colleagues and not least, bad for the individual. Make sure that your staff can operate safely from the outset.

You may want to consider whether to ask top executives to introduce the course, so that newcomers meet them and feel valued by them. This demonstrates their commitment to the course and to the newcomers. You may also wish to consider giving any recognised unions a 'spot' on the course so that they can tell potential members about what they offer.

Much information, such as that on company products, will be forgotten if given on the first day, even for those who need it, ie sales people. There is reduced recall in the early stages owing to the anxiety and stress (as well as excitement) of a new job. This information is rarely crucial so usually it can wait until the formal induction course, and one of the later sessions if the programme is modular.

Employee benefits, contractual details and appraisal are usually covered in detail so that newcomers know what is expected of them and how they can benefit. The company sells itself again by showing newcomers what they can gain by working for the company, reinforcing their decision to join.

Other factors you may wish to consider include:

- Should information be given on the industry as well as the company?
- Can some skills training, for which there is a common need, be given too?
- Does the induction course introduce the newcomers to role models?
- Can some of the course be made humorous? (Laughter often aids memory.)
- Can inductees watch company advertisements, and discuss them (rather than the tired lecture approach to company image and products)? Can they see real examples of the products?
- A session asking the inductees to talk about why they joined (to reinforce their commitment to the company).

If the course cannot be run in regular modules (six times two hours being better than two full days), the induction 'day(s)' should be short, recognising the limited recall at the start of the job and the overload of information.

Consider also the likely starting point for the trainees, and what level they are already at, before determining the training material.

Learning styles and training methods

Learning theory

A great deal has been written about the way people learn, and a huge amount of research has been conducted on it. A synopsis of some of the main points, as they are relevant to designing an induction course, is given here. Further reading is suggested for those who wish to study this area further (see pages 155–57).

Learning is a key process in human behaviour, influencing everything we do and everything we think. It is a relatively permanent change of behaviour, for better or worse, which usually takes place through experience or practice. This section is mainly concerned with the acquisition of knowledge and skills, though, as noted in Chapter 2, the question of attitudes and values is important, as it helps to shape the individual's 'behavioural contract'. Knowledge and skills can be developed in others, but it is quite difficult to bring about a change in other people's attitudes.

People vary in how they learn. Most people show a mix of 'learning styles'. Questionnaires enabling people to determine their preferred learning styles are commercially available, and categorise people by four main learning styles (Figure 5.1). The questionnaires give only a broad indication of learning style and are based on self-analysis. Most people favour one style but they may score fairly high on others. However, the broad indication is useful, and demonstrates that any induction course should try to ensure that people of all learning styles will benefit.

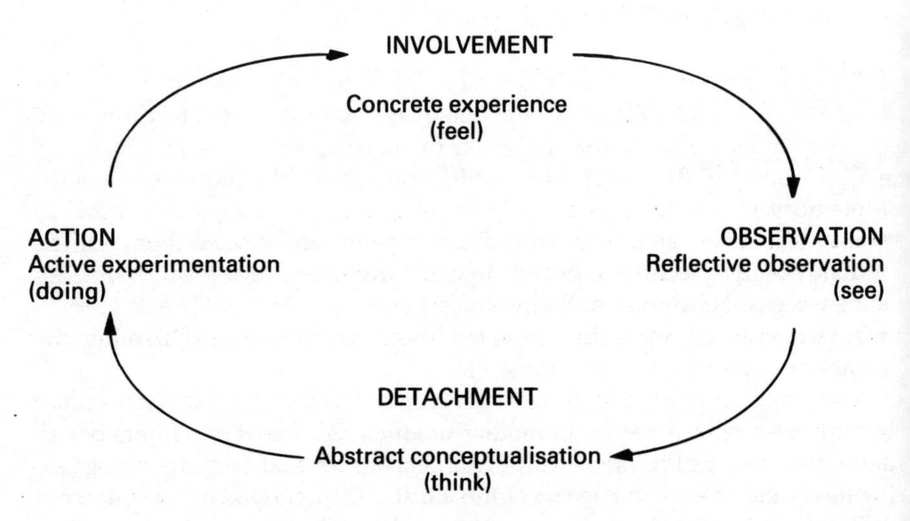

Figure 5.1. *Learning style inventory*

The learning styles are:

(a) *Concrete experience*. This can be thought of as learning by feeling. It shows a receptive, experience-based approach to learning, where judgements are influenced by how the individual feels. People who score highly on this tend to be empathic and people-orientated. They find theoretical approaches unhelpful and learn best from using specific examples, treating each as a unique case and becoming involved in it. They benefit most from feedback and discussion with others with similar learning preferences.

(b) *Active experimentation.* This can be thought of as learning by doing. People who score highly on active experimentation prefer learning through action, engaging in projects and small group discussions. They find lectures and other passive forms of learning unhelpful.

(c) *Abstract conceptualisation.* This can be thought of as learning by thinking. It represents an analytical, theoretical approach, relying on logical thinking and rational evaluation. People who score highly on this tend to be more concerned with things and symbols than with other people. Impersonal learning situations emphasising systematic analysis suit them best. They become frustrated and benefit little from unstructured 'discovery' exercises and simulations which the active experimenters favour.

(d) *Reflective observation.* This can be thought of as learning by watching. Reflective observers have a tentative, objective and reflective approach. They rely on careful observations in making judgements and favour lectures and films, which allow them to remain impartial.

Induction training should cater for different learning styles through the use of different training methods.

Training methods

Most induction training is about *giving* information. Turning this round to suit different learning styles so that at least some of it is presented for the individuals or groups to *discover* may be beneficial. Also, the trainer or supervisor should give the individuals a chance to give information too – what they can do, what they are good at and why they wanted to join the company.

Training should be tailored to individual capacities, and is easier if similar groups and grades of new recruits are banded together. Obvious differences, such as the needs of people with disabilities, ethnic minorities, women returners, school leavers, etc should be taken into account (more on this in Chapter 6). Less obvious are differences in company cultures, such as those experienced when changing from a small company to a multinational – this is an aspect that should be picked up by the supervisor for individual attention.

Some induction courses use 'treasure hunt' type games. Inductees are set exercises and given questions to help them find out about the company, and present these to their colleagues at the next session. This method is sometimes seen as 'studenty'; it can be particularly useful for school and college leavers who are used to this kind of situation, but it may be best avoided for those who are liable to feel less confident initially, such as women returners, and consideration should be given to how much of their own time this would take, particularly for part-timers.

If the course is flexible enough, you may wish to get the new starters to fill in the learning styles questionnaire so that you can tailor the training directly to their needs.

Self-managed learning
Self-managed learning must be supported. Induction usually takes place through a number of meetings where the newcomers arrange all or part of their own training, including the induction course itself.

New employees may be asked to arrange the speakers for the next induction session, and organise their own programme – this type of induction training has been successfully used for new graduate trainees. One advantage of this method is that inductees are free of the usual limitations and taboos. They may approach speakers normally considered too important or busy to be asked, either within or outside the company.

Projects arising from self-managed learning can include quality improvement projects. Successes bolster their achievements and productivity may increase markedly as they do not learn 'what you can't do around here'. The individuals can gain enhanced visibility with senior managers and key contacts, but this may be at the price of the envy of other staff. A further problem, particularly for new graduates (see the next chapter), is that the induction programme may seem more exciting than the job if they are being given work which they consider below their capabilities.

Self-managed learning groups often become highly cohesive and the staff turnover for them is low. However, they may not integrate well with other groups.

Once you have decided on the content, consider how this should be given to the new starters. If you are able to design an induction course to run in several two- or three-hour blocks, the benefit is likely to be greater than if the induction course runs across one or two full days. You will also be able to intersperse the material with work, linking it to what they will be doing each day. This would also enable them to have time to manage their own learning – they could research different topics (one each, or in groups) and present their findings to the rest of the group at the next meeting.

Training aids

The list below gives a short description of some of the training aids that can be used. Remember that you should choose a training aid appropriate to the material to be covered. It is important that you know what you are aiming to achieve by the use of your chosen medium.

Films and videos
These are useful for:

- showing less accessible parts of the company, such as sites overseas, or showing parts of the factories to white collar workers, etc
- introducing the chairman/woman of the company

- showing commercial advertisements for the company
- illustrating graphs of financial results, making them 'come alive' by showing how the results are derived, and from what part of the business.

The disadvantages are that inductees can sleep peacefully through the film if it is boring! Films and videos are expensive to produce and are likely to date quickly, but the visual impact is strong and likely to be remembered.

Tape/slide packs
Cheaper than videos, these can be updated more easily, by replacing old slides and re-recording the soundtrack, if any. They are very flexible as all or part of the pack can be shown, and it is easy to flip backwards or forwards in the programme to answer questions or illustrate particular points. As the room is usually darkened for tape/slide packs, the 'sleep' problem (see films) is also possible.

Overhead projector slides (OHPs)
Probably one of the most common visual aids, these can supplement lectures and are flexible and cheap to produce. Dangers are too much information crowded on to the acetates or their being unreadable owing to bad focusing, etc.

Visits and tours of buildings
You may need to provide a map, or send a search party for stragglers, but visits are good for showing the reality of the company, rather than 'glossy handouts' or carefully stage-managed films. Visits mean that the inductees will see other people working as well as other parts of the company, and will build up a catalogue of familiar faces. Sometimes, with a small group, you can stop to talk to other workers on the way, asking them for views or practical demonstrations of their work. This is useful for learning about the work only, not for helping them to remember names!

Discussion groups and case studies
These are useful for illustrating the reasons for company policies. Groups can be used to discuss company values such as customer care and quality, and for giving newcomers a chance to express their views on the company advertising (particularly their recruitment advertisements) and suggest other improvements to the business.

Discussions supplementing case studies can be used to consider issues or show them a particular mode of behaviour, such as what to do if a colleague is shirking their duties, or how racial harassment cases would be handled, or for problem-solving exercises illustrating company values.

Guest speakers
In-company specialists are used to talking about the company and/or various functions. Using speakers who are top managers in the organisation will give them visibility and show the newcomers that they are interested in them.

It will be useful to rotate the speakers to avoid taking up too much of their time and to ensure that they do not become stale.

Tests and questionnaires
Some companies use tests and questionnaires to check learning and recall of information already given. However, these can provoke further anxieties if the newcomers worry about failing. Tests will be necessary in some areas for safety reasons. The 'treasure hunt' is a variant of this method. One American health-care company uses questions from new recruits to prime talks from the top executive. Each new starter is asked what they would ask if they could ask the managing director one question. The questions are then given to the MD before his or her speech to the newcomers, so that points can be answered.

Computer-based training
This is useful, if the equipment is available, for familiarising newcomers with new technology, for keyboard training and for interactive question and answer programmes, though these need facilitation and back-up material. Information about the company may also be kept in computer information files. This method of training can be very effective, but it relies on well-motivated individuals as they may be unsupervised. Conversely, this means that they can fit in training when they are less busy and have more time.

Simulations
These can be used with great effect when teaching how to use fire extinguishers, etc. A small fire can be started in a safe, sheltered place, with qualified firefighters looking on, and individuals practise putting out the fire.

Group simulation games can show individual strengths and weaknesses, eg on analytical and decision-making skills, social skills, co-operativeness and leadership potential, which can give indications of further training needed. If well controlled they can be predictive of job performance. However, the motivation of the losing team may drop and these games are only really possible where there are large numbers of new recruits.

Company literature
No course is complete without it! Loose-leaf folders are useful so that new employees can supplement the written material with their own notes. Well-designed company literature should build on the information the new-comers saw at the recruitment stage. The material should include charts, diagrams and colour pictures and be well laid out with good use of white space. It should be eye-catching as this is the easiest training material to ignore. Old photocopies of out-of-date organisation charts will not impress newcomers, or show them that they matter. Complicated procedures may be better explained by the use of flow charts in many instances, rather than dense paragraphs of text.

Information should be presented so that it is understandable – converted sales literature can be good, as it often uses simple language and demonstrates the benefits of the products convincingly.

Try to ensure that newcomers do not simply receive a huge pile of material that all looks the same. Even coloured pages can help to break up the monotony.

Location of the course

Where the training is held is also important. If the venue is away from the usual premises, a map should be provided together with details of how to get there.

The venue should be undisturbed, so that newcomers are not tempted back to the workplace to get on with 'urgent' work. Where possible the induction course should be held somewhere bright and airy. Wallcharts, screens and OHPs should be visible from all around the room. Treat inductees as you would treat customers. They should be free of phone calls, pagers, etc but a message service can be provided. If people with disabilities are to attend, make sure that the venue is adequately equipped to cater for their needs, ie with good wheelchair access, hearing aid loops, and interpreters or deaf language signers available, etc.

If there is a large group of new employees, sit them around tables in groups of six to eight. They will get to know each other more quickly than if they were en masse (the socialisation element is important) and discussion groups are ready-made.

It is customary to provide a good lunch if running single days, usually with vegetarian options these days, but avoiding alcohol. A pre-course programme sent to participants can ask about any special dietary requirements, either for health or religious reasons or personal preference. The lunch helps to motivate people to attend and to look forward to the course, as rumours of 'at least you will eat well' travel!

Piloting the course

Courses should be piloted or tested, even with just one or two 'guinea pigs', before launching them on the new starters. Despite careful design, material can be ambiguous or not properly linked with the experience in the workplace. Piloting will help to ensure that:

- the course is well structured and all the content is covered (nothing inadvertently left out)
- that the content 'fits' together
- that the recipients feel treated as adults rather than as schoolchildren
- that the proposed speakers (and their 'understudies') are competent, and talk about the right subjects
- that paperwork is properly and suitably packaged, and builds on the recruitment literature

- that it gives a good company image
- that it avoids overselling the job or promotion prospects (unless carefully explained, videos of overseas offices may lead people to think that they could work or visit there)
- that the timing of the sessions works (particularly where a tour of the site or a factory visit is arranged)
- time is allowed for the recruits to ask questions.

Once the course has been tried out, any amendments can be made and it can be delivered to new recruits. However, the course should be monitored closely and evaluated frequently. (See also Chapter 8.)

Translating learning theory into practice

Learning must be structured and systematically planned for optimum learning conditions. Old-fashioned reliance on 'sitting by Nellie' or on 'chalk and talk' is not enough.

Any skill learning should involve practice over a longer period, in short bursts. Feedback and encouragement should be given; encouragement is a psychological reward.

Patience in giving complete job performance information and training greatly increases the opportunity for learning to occur.

Skill acquisition and job training

How skill is acquired may be a factor in the induction course, if it is to include skills training, eg typing, learning crafts, etc, and will certainly be relevant for on-the-job training and coaching.

The acquisition of skills is usually active. Frequency of repetition is important in ensuring retention of the skill. Positive reinforcement, in the form of rewards and successes, is usually more effective than negative reinforcement, punishment and failure.

Motivation to learn

People need goals to learn quickly and effectively. A motivated person learns more quickly than an unmotivated one. For motivation to be retained, the goals must be achievable and early rewards reinforce better than delayed ones. Motivation can be intrinsic, learning for the pleasure of it, simply from the desire to master the skill, or it can be extrinsic, wanting to learn for the sake of external rewards.

Knowledge of results through feedback is very important. Although the trainee may be able to see the results, for instance if welding, it is also useful to give praise and encouragement, together with information to convince the trainee that it is normal not to be able to master the skill instantly. In cases where the individual may not be able to see the results, feedback and reassurance are even more important.

Specific feedback should be given in 'manageable chunks' so that the learner is not overloaded with information. (Driving instructors usually ask their clients to try to remember just a couple of points at a time, otherwise they find that they cannot remember any.)

Skill development

Development of skilled performance passes through three stages:

(a) *The cognitive phase,* where attempts are made to analyse tasks and verbalise what is being learned. What to do and what to expect are emphasised, procedures are described and information given about typical errors. This varies in complexity according to the tasks.
(b) *The associative phase,* where correct patterns of behaviour are practised and begin to become established. Errors are gradually eliminated.
(c) *The autonomous stage,* where the skill becomes automatic. Speed of performance increases and errors reduce. There is also increasing resistance to stress and to interference from other activities.

Learning curves

The change in behaviour and increase in skill level can be plotted on a graph against time, creating a curve. Different activities and different people have different shaped curves, of different lengths.

The duration of the training needed will depend on the tasks and on the initial level of the trainee's ability. Most curves show fast initial learning (the initial 'spurt'), partly owing to the fact that it is easier to learn from a low starting point.

For complex tasks, the learning curve will include plateaux, where time goes by but learning temporarily stops. The trainee may feel overloaded and dispirited. Where a plateau occurs, changing the teaching method may help – there is no value in being 'stuck' if this can be avoided, as progress is not being made and the trainee's motivation is likely to decrease. At the end of a plateau, new learning begins again and incorrect learning or 'bad habits' are eliminated.

The curve in Figure 5.2, showing several plateaux, is typical of that experienced when learning to drive or type, etc.

Planning and delivering training

Training can be 'distributed' (little and often) or 'massed' (in one lump). Distribution of learning is usually better for learning and retaining physical skills than for verbal learning. The less meaningful the material and the greater its difficulty and quantity, the greater the benefit from distributed practice.

Translating this to the induction programme, it is better to arrange several short sessions over a number of weeks. Information about the company

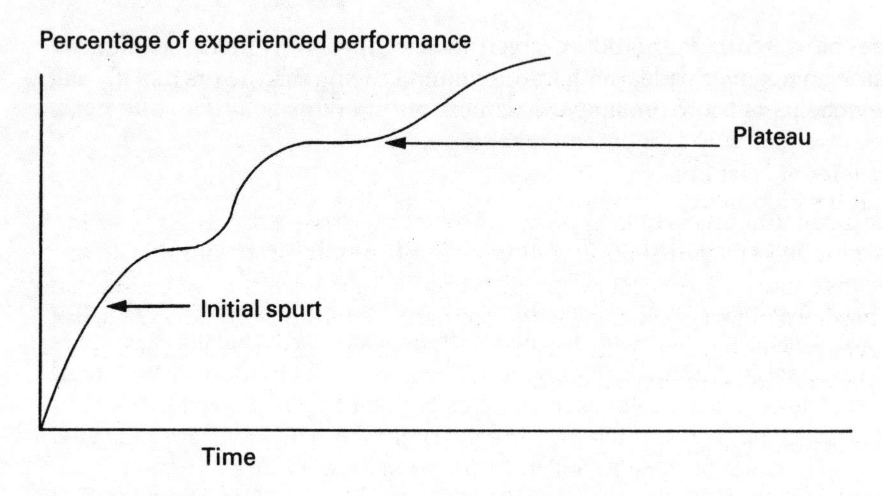

Figure 5.2. *Complex learning curve with plateaux*

(verbal learning) can be given in longer sessions, in one go. However, too much information can still overload individuals at the beginning of a new job, when they are still anxious about the company and their own performance.

Depending on the complexity and the organisation of the material, it may be better to break it down into related segments (parts) rather than try to teach it as a whole. Table 5.1 shows the relationship between part or whole learning and the organisation and complexity.

Table 5.1. *Whole versus part learning*

	Complexity	
Organisation	High	Low
High	Whole methods superior	Part method better 75% of the time
Low	Part method superior 63% of the time	Part and whole methods equally successful

The total length of the task and the number of elements involved must be considered. The more intelligent the trainee, the more likely the whole method will be best (as they prefer to see the 'big picture'). Also, if training is distributed rather than massed, whole learning will be better.

Material learned in parts should be given in the correct sequence, otherwise learning one part may interfere with learning another, or there may be a temptation to put the parts in the wrong order. Another disadvantage of part learning is the time taken to relink (or recap) on the previous parts before making the whole.

Transfer of learning

The aim of training is to help people learn transferable skills, eg transferring learning of keyboard skills on a typewriter to a word processor. However, negative transfer also occurs, lengthening the time taken for the individual to become proficient, such as when old habits interfere with new ones and previous skills have to be 'unlearned' – for instance, when trying to master a keyboard with a different layout.

Memory and recall

When designing an induction course or organising skills training, note that memory can be unreliable. Expecting people to recall a mass of information is not realistic unless they can see prompts. The problem becomes worse if you are expecting them to convey the message to others, creating distortions in the message (similar to those produced in the children's game 'Chinese Whispers').

Research has shown that when people were read a story and then asked to retell it, the story shortened each time, as only the main details were recalled. Beginnings and endings remained fairly intact, but much of the detail was lost, and the details retained were usually personalised, so that they remembered things that they themselves associated with.

In general people recall only about 40 per cent of what they hear. This means that if only oral instructions or messages are to be given, they will need to be repeated.

Reasons for inaccuracy of recall include:

(a) Observation is inaccurate in the first place, and details are omitted.
(b) Perception may influence observation and recall.
(c) Unintentional elaboration or embellishments may occur (particularly if they forget or only half-remember a part, and then fill the gap with guesswork).
(d) People can be misled by suggestions.
(e) People may be motivated to forget – perhaps the learning is unpleasant, or reminds them of experiences or feelings they wish to forget.

For information to be recalled it should be meaningful. There are many instances where people are introduced to someone, then promptly forget their name. This is because the name had no connection with them, and interest and motivation were insufficient.

If the information you wish to convey is complex or important, notes should be given. Flow diagrams and information 'trees' also aid memory and understanding because the links can be seen. If these notes would be useful to them in their work, you may wish to consider training the inductees in mind-mapping techniques so that they can build models of the information.

Induction manuals and employees' log books

It can be useful to create an induction manual so that you do not lose the expertise. It will require regular updating but can document feedback and comments, showing why some things were not tried, and what was successful and unsuccessful and why. If there is high staff turnover in certain grades, the induction programme for that group can be amended in line with any comments at exit interviews.

The induction manual also provides information from which any new group can run the programme – in a large organisation it is not just the new starters who keep changing!

A log book can also be created for new employees, setting out information to be covered during the induction period and allowing the supervisor to initial or sign off each stage when those job skills have been learned or pieces of information have been explained and understood. Comments on observations and measurements of the job can also be added. This provides the company with a record showing that the induction has been carried out, and the employee with a reminder of the areas covered.

Advice can be sought from new employees on how they would like to see the log book set out.

Induction course checklist

1. Have you decided on a formal induction course?
2. Have you thought about the who, what, when, where and how?
3. Have you gained senior management commitment and agreed a budget?
4. Have you decided on the course objectives, content and timetable?
5. Have you thought about the training methods to be used?
6. Have you secured the necessary training aids and invited speakers, etc and found an appropriate venue?
7. Have you piloted the course and made any necessary adjustments?
8. Have you given clear information to course delegates on where to go, the duration and what to expect? Does the pre-course material tie in with information they have already had and reflect well on the organisation?
9. Have you helped the newcomer to learn job skills and overcome learning plateaux by arranging training in manageable amounts, at the right level?
10. Have you provided a log book so that the newcomer's progress can be documented?

5.1 Trainer/administrator's checklist for an induction course

Before the course:

1. Check venue booked/organised; ensure that it is wheelchair accessible or has hearing aid loops, etc, if necessary.
2. Check refreshments ordered/booked.
3. Check facilities, eg flip charts, video/TVs, OHPs, projectors ordered, etc.
4. Check domestic arrangements.
5. Prepare pre-course materials.
6. Prepare handouts, visual aids (and check that they will be visible), etc.
7. Invite course members and give/send pre-course information.
8. Invite speakers and give details of what they should talk about, at what time and for how long, prime back-up speakers in the same way (in case of sickness).
9. Pack trainer's box to take to venue, including:
   - visual aids – OHPs, slides, videos, wallcharts, etc (two sets just in case some walk!)
   - other props, eg examples of products or sales literature
   - handouts and written materials
   - trainer's notes
   - writing materials – pens and paper, etc
   - flip chart pens
   - spare OHP acetates
   - sticky tape/masking tape
   - Blu-Tack
   - drawing pins (in a box!)
   - scissors
   - hole puncher for handouts
   - badges (delegates and trainers) and/or blank nameplates
   - copy of joining instructions/pre-course brochure issued to delegates.
10. Take/arrange for transport of trainer's box to the venue.

On the morning of the course:

1. Check electrical sockets/equipment – ensure that it is working properly.
2. Check contents of trainer's box.
3. Check seating arrangements for delegates (if a large group is arranged in smaller groups of six to eight around tables, the small discussion groups are already formed; also helps people to socialise).
4. Check that water, nameplates, information folders and writing materials are laid out for delegates.

5. Organise/lay out visual aids for easy use and identification.
6. Check that flip chart pens are working (not dried up).
7. Ensure that people at the back can see visual aids, nothing blocking the view, aids are large enough.
8. Double-check with venue on times of refreshments and that messages will be taken.
9. Organise/lay out handouts so they can be identified easily.
10. Lay out any course brochures, other literature.
11. Check location of fire exits and assembly points and toilets.
12. Organise registration – complete badges and check off course members.
13. Sort out any last-minute dietary changes.

Checklist for 'welcome' to course members:

1. Say 'welcome'.
2. Check registration complete and they are all there for induction training.
3. Tell them about domestic arrangements, eg location of fire exits, assembly points and toilets, no phone calls but messages brought, turn off pagers, where they can telephone from, house rules on smoking, what cannot be put on to expenses (if in a hotel).
4. Remind them of programme – what is in store, timings and when breaks are.
5. Congratulate them on joining the company – give them information on the percentages of people who are selected to reinforce the idea that the company really wants them.
6. Introductions – give format for introductions, either working in pairs and introducing each other to the group or introducing themselves if time is short; introductions should cover:
   - name and department
   - how long they have worked for the company
   - why they joined (to remind them of the benefits and reinforce it as the right choice)
   - what they hope to gain from the course
   - something they fear
   - something unusual about themselves (last two to break the ice and give them something other than work to talk about during the first break).

During the day:

1. Let them stretch every now and then, particularly if they are not otherwise moving around.

2. Suggest they swap telephone numbers with two others and arrange to contact them again in a month to see how they are doing (two better than one in case one forgets, three may seem too many).
3. Make sure they get any messages.
4. Ensure they don't get lost!

At the end of the course:

1. Remind them to remove all their belongings.
2. Give them evaluation/review forms to complete.

5.2 Letter inviting newcomers to the induction course

On letterheaded paper

Dear (name to be written in)

I am very pleased to welcome you to (company name)'s induction course on (date) at (location) starting at (start time).

In order to ensure that you gain as much as possible from the course, I enclose some information about the content of the course together with a list of other course delegates and a map showing routes and details of access.

Except for emergencies no telephone calls will be allowed during the sessions, but messages will be delivered during breaks.

You will be given a badge when you arrive and register – please wear this so that other course members may identify you. This will also enable training staff to locate you more easily when delivering messages.

You will be given documentation during the programme, but writing materials will also be provided so that you may take your own notes if you wish.

Food provided during the course will include vegetarian options. Please let me know at least 48 hours before the course if you have any other particular dietary requirements.

At the end of the course you will be given a questionnaire to enable us to ascertain your opinions of the programme. We would be very grateful if you would take the time to complete this and hand it in at the registration desk before leaving. This important source of information enables us to monitor and improve the course.

I hope that you enjoy the induction course and will benefit from it.

Yours sincerely,

(Name)
(Title)

5.3 Induction course details and programme

1. Course objectives
   On completion, course members should:
   (a) be aware of the organisation and structure of (company name)
   (b) be aware of the roles, functions and main responsibilities of each of the main divisions/departments
   (c) have a good understanding of (company name)'s history
   (d) have a good understanding of the main products and be able to name the main customers and competitors
   (e) understand the terms and conditions, rules and procedures applying to their employment
   (f) appreciate the facilities and services available to assist in carrying out their work effectively.

2. Course methods
   Lectures, discussion groups, presentations, videos, visiting speakers

3. Syllabus
   (a) Introduction to (company name)
   (b) Mission, aims and values
   (c) History and organisation structure
   (d) Products/services, customers, suppliers and competitors
   (e) Terms and conditions of employment, including:

   - pay, pay increases and expenses
   - the grading structure
   - probationary period and appraisal
   - promotion and transfers
   - discipline
   - leave and sickness absence
   - the pension scheme
   - other benefits

   (f) Safety and security
   (g) Office services
   (h) Recreational facilities
   (i) Further training and developments
   (j) Staff associations.

5.4 Traditional induction course timetable with associated case study exercise

Day 1

09.00 – 09.15	Registration and coffee
09.15 – 09.45	General welcome and introductions
09.45 – 10.15	History and organisation structure (lecture with OHPs, handouts, hierarchy charts, list of who's who)
10.15 – 10.45	Video – overview of company – shows locations, functions and people working in them, manufacturing processes, quality team, company products/services, opportunities
10.45 – 11.00	Coffee
11.00 – 11.15	Mission, aims, values – as illustrated by film (lecture with OHPs and handouts)
11.15 – 12.00	Discussion group(s) on quality – what does it mean to the newcomers? What is the customer entitled to expect? What is the last thing the customer wants? How do individual contributions make an impact on quality?
12.00 – 12.30	Overview of products/services – what do we do/make and where? What manufacturing processes are involved? (lecture with slides and handouts – flow diagrams for processes)
12.30 – 13.30	Lunch
13.30 – 14.15	Video of company adverts – discussion of relationship between products, quality, processes, individual contribution, customer and company profit
14.15 – 15.15	Safety and security – company and individual responsibilities, fire – dangers, where it starts, extinguishers, etc – first aid points/procedures, hazardous processes, computer security, other security (lecture with OHPs and handouts, fire officer visiting)
15.15 – 15.30	Tea
15.30 – 16.45	Practical session – putting out fires (held at far outpost of buildings, fire officers attending)

Day 2

09.30 – 10.00	Terms and conditions – what the main clauses cover (lecture with OHPs and handouts)
10.00 – 10.30	Case study – fair employment, in groups
10.30 – 10.45	Coffee
10.45 – 11.15	Plenary – feedback on discussion of case study
11.15 – 12.15	Grading structure, pay – payslips, when, how, etc. Expenses – how to claim, what is allowed (lecture with OHPs and handouts)
12.15 – 13.00	Probationary period, appraisal and how work is assessed linking to case study, what on-the-job training to expect (lecture and discussion, OHPs, handouts)
13.00 – 14.00	Lunch
14.00 – 14.15	Discipline – what's allowed and why, links with safety – what do they think? (quick-fire, wake-them-up questions)
14.15 – 15.00	Promotion, transfers, discipline – fairness issues and equal opportunities, how to discipline – procedures (lecture, OHP, handouts)
15.00 – 15.15	Tea
15.15 – 15.45	Recreational facilities (talk from recreational organiser)
15.45 – 17.00	Group brainstorming – what other conditions are there? What benefits are offered? – including sickness, holidays, other leave, pensions, cars, health care, etc. Link to case study – what should a good employer offer? (with handouts)

Day 3

09.30 – 10.00	Problems – what to do, grievance procedure, equal opportunities, welfare (lecture with handouts)
10.00 – 10.45	Training and development, how internal posts are advertised and how to get the best out of your job, eg importance of admitting you don't know and asking questions (lecture with handouts)

10.45 – 11.00	Coffee
11.00 – 11.30	Office services – where to find the things you need, what the support functions do, in-company communications (lecture with handouts)
11.30 – 12.30	Brainstorming – what do they think they know about the company so far?
12.30 – 13.30	Lunch
13.30 – 15.00	Presentations (15 minutes each) from six heads of department about what their sections do
15.00 – 15.30	Tea
15.30 – 16.15	Questions to panel of presenters (heads of department) from the newcomers on any aspect of the company or terms and conditions, etc
16.15 – 16.30	Course evaluation
16.30	Course ends

Case study used in induction course

You and your group have formed a company and want to discuss how to organise and treat your staff. Model your fictitious company on (a smaller version of) the one you have just joined.

1. What do you think is a fair way of deciding an employee's pay?
   How would pay rises be determined?
2. What would be a fair way of monitoring the work performance of your staff?
   How would you make sure this happened properly?
   What issues would you want to take into account?
3. What would you do to help a new member of staff settle in and become effective quickly?
   What would you do if their performance just failed to reach a satisfactory standard?
4. What guidance do you want to offer your staff in terms of fairness and equal opportunities?
   What areas of employment do you think should be covered by this?
5. A member of staff comes back from lunch one day smelling of drink. He is abusive to the supervisor and is operating machinery without a guard. What should happen? What would you do?

6. One of your longer-serving staff keeps taking days off, coming in late and leaving early.
   How would you investigate?
   What do you think is a fair way of tackling the problem?
7. Your company has been in business for some while, quite successfully, and you now want to be able to offer your staff something more.
   What do you think a good employer should offer in terms of benefits?
   Which will be valuable to the staff but also cost-effective for you to provide?

Chapter 6

Catering for Particular Needs

This chapter examines the particular needs of various distinct groups of workers, and special needs for special situations. It will be possible to build some of these into a formal induction programme, particularly where similar types of employee are grouped together, but will particularly influence informal training in the workplace.

People with disabilities

Although it may seem obvious, all disabilities are not the same, and people with disabilities are as varied as any other group of workers. This section makes no distinction between those people who are registered disabled and those who are not, and it also covers special medical needs. If your workers are to be productive, special needs should be catered for as far as possible.

The most important thing to discover is the exact nature of the disability, how it manifests itself in terms of the individual's capabilities for work and what particular special needs are relevant. A great number of people think only of wheelchairs and wheelchair access when disabilities are mentioned, but needs can vary enormously even between different people with (say) cerebral palsy or epilepsy. There are huge differences, too, in the needs of those with mental and physical disabilities.

The best advice is to ask the individuals themselves what they need. In the vast majority of cases they will be helpful and accommodating. Specialist advice is also available from Disablement Resettlement Officers, who can be contacted through your local Jobcentre, and from RADAR, the Royal Association for Disabilities and Rehabilitation. Advice and information are available on equipment, such as

- wheelchair access to buildings and toilets, etc
- arrangement for and provision of hearing loops
- transcription of information into braille
- large-scale computer screens and keyboards for those with poor vision
- finding deaf/dumb signers
- grants for special pieces of equipment, etc.

RADAR also produces a book for employers categorising the disabilities, the kind of problems encountered and advice on dealing with them.

There will naturally be ongoing special needs, not just for induction, but to ensure that individuals can escape quickly in case of fire, etc. This may mean that another person should be made responsible for alerting them if they are unable to hear a fire alarm, or helping to lead them out if they cannot see the way down the unfamiliar fire stairs. Fire departments can also offer advice here.

Similarly there may be ongoing first aid needs, so that other employees understand how to deal with insulin shock or epileptic fits, for instance.

Those with mental disabilities may have special needs for induction (and for work) including short sessions, as concentration may be impaired or they may worry more. As before, take advice about their needs.

The popular conception of people with disabilities being unhealthy is not borne out by research. Typically, people with disabilities take less sick leave than others, and are often loyal and enthusiastic workers. Although they may have disabilities in some areas, it is often much more productive to concentrate on the things that they *can* do rather than those they cannot.

Part-timers and shift-workers

Part-timers, job sharers and shift-workers are often forgotten when designing induction courses, as the usual assumption is that all employees are around for all the usual (office) working hours. This is obviously not so, and special arrangements should be made to ensure that these groups of people get enough and adequate induction training. If everyone else is addressed by the company chairman, they should be too, even if it takes a little more organisation.

Induction courses should be organised so that part-timers or shift-workers do not have to attend in their own time, even if they are paid overtime. Full-time workers are not expected to give up their leisure time to attend, nor should others be. If there is absolutely no way round asking for their attendance outside their normal hours, they should be well compensated for this, including any extras they might have to pay for childminding costs, etc.

The time taken for shift- and part-time workers to absorb training and understand and master the job may appear to be slightly longer than for full-timers. This is because there are usually longer breaks between the learning periods. Effective feedback on performance will help to make up for the lack of continuity. You may wish to increase the probationary period for these groups to compensate.

During induction for part-time workers, you will need to pay greater attention to the contract of employment, as even pro-rata conditions are not always as straightforward as they seem and it is important for both parties that these are understood. Job-sharers should understand what happens when their 'partner' is on holiday – in some cases employers want them to become full time during those periods. Similarly, the issue of what happens if the other job-sharer leaves should be thoroughly aired and understood. Supervisors will also need to agree exactly how the work can be split or shared, ie whether the job description is similar for both or if some duties are assigned to one of the job descriptions and some to the other.

Because these people are not around all the time, there is a danger that they can feel left out and isolated. Unlike other workers, each time they come in to work, things are not as they left them – the work has moved on. This alone takes some adjustment for those not used to it. Part-timers and job-sharers often miss important meetings, so it is a good idea to make someone responsible for ensuring that they get all the information everyone else does.

Distant workers and professionals

Distant workers include sales representatives, travelling repair and maintenance staff, health visitors, homeworkers, lighthouse keepers, etc who work alone and away from the main site of the organisation, and those whose group is distant, such as oil rig workers or regional office staff. There are many people who will fall into this category, but the amount of contact they have with their head office base may be quite different.

Ideally, they should have a place where they can work when they are in the office, even if this is shared with others who spend most of their time away from the base. All need to understand their commitments to attend meetings, etc and to ensure that they are in contact with their managers or supervisors so that problems can be dealt with and their performance monitored.

Regular progress checks are essential; it is easy for managers to lose control completely if their subordinates are constantly out of the office and managers have little idea of what they are doing. It is also much more useful for the newcomer to gain feedback on how they are doing.

Workers who are distant from the main work location can experience problems of isolation, and induction for them is particularly important and needs to be more thorough – they cannot simply 'pop next door' to find answers to questions. It may be useful to run induction courses for distant workers together, so that they can build up good contacts with their peers and provide a support network for each other.

Special emphasis should be placed on the need to make them feel part of the company rather than isolated from it. A strong sense of belonging helps sales representatives to withstand the loneliness of solo lunches at roadside caravans and contact mainly with clients who may be strangers.

The induction process should enable them to understand what expenses can be claimed and how often they are expected to telephone the office, the procedure for reporting if they are sick and when they can act on their own initiative, eg getting car repairs sorted out immediately, rather than having to wait for authorisation, to enable them to travel to see clients the next day.

In some cases tradespeople are paired with 'old hands' to 'show them the ropes'. This helps the new recruit to learn the job and build up contacts, but care should be taken to ensure that any bad habits are not passed on. As with any other new starter, it is the manager's responsibility to make sure that training is adequate and effective and that performance is in line with the job requirements.

Many professionals share similarities with distant workers. Although usually on the company premises, they often work mainly alone even if nominally in a team. Their role is often advisory or they may act as internal consultants, not actually belonging to any one team but being a resource for all. Often they are equipped with qualifications which necessitate no further job training – they are seen to be able to do the job from day one. Examples of this include lawyers, doctors, architects and engineers. As they already possess the qualifications for the job the organisation often gives them no induction. They do not have to be tested on their job skills or win professional credibility (which is usually taken for granted unless there are strong contra-indications) and their need to understand the organisation, the people and the environment is largely ignored.

Women returners

There has been much discussion of the current demographic dip and the subsequent encouragement of women to return to work after raising their families. However, women may lack confidence on returning as technology has probably changed radically since they left the workplace some years ago. They may feel that they will have difficulty in re-learning this and office routines. Although they may have good, useful and transferable skills in the home, such as budgetary capabilities, they seldom feel that these are valued in the workplace.

Updating training should be given so that new skills can be learned or revitalised. Those who have undertaken specific 'women returner' courses are likely to find that benefits include rebuilding their confidence and renewing their skills.

Working practices may also have changed – even in small ways, such as the increased likelihood of everyone being addressed by their forename rather than title and surname. The culture may have changed so that the whole environment has become less hierarchical. If women return to the same company where they last worked, they may find that former colleagues have risen in the system, and that old friends are no longer peers but their bosses, which can be difficult to adjust to.

Women returning to work may have the increased pressure of beginning a new job while carrying guilt and worry about leaving their children and whether they are doing the right thing. They may also be worrying about the quality of their childminder.

Returners may also be unused to working in teams, with their former associates being mainly other mothers and children rather than mixed groups of people of all ages.

Women returners are more likely to respond to specific individual job tuition than group-based training, where their peers can see their progress. Depending on how long they have been away from work, and their own individual level, the baseline from which they will learn and re-learn will differ. The whole job and its context will need explanation to ensure a full understanding, but this should be done unpatronisingly and flexibly, so that where it is obvious that a good grasp of the area already exists they can progress to another.

Ethnic minorities

Differences in language, background, culture, religious beliefs, social conventions and traditions may be apparent in the groups who constitute the workforce. It is important to show that racial bias or harassment will not be tolerated and that everyone is respected and considered equal.

It may be useful to discuss the differences and how practices of other cultures can be accepted into the workplace; for example, if some people need to say regular prayers throughout the day, aside from the work, their breaks may be arranged to accommodate this. Discussion can help everyone's understanding so that colleagues do not inadvertently behave or speak in a way which upsets people with different origins or beliefs.

Differences in dietary requirements may be accommodated by the staff canteen and on any formal induction course, if there is one, and periods of fasting taken into account. Where tea or coffee are not drunk, soft drinks can be provided. These things involve very little effort yet can make a difference in helping the newcomer to integrate in what may be for them a slightly different culture.

Language training may be given where appropriate and race equality training for supervisors and managers. It is particularly important that bias is avoided in the immediate manager of the individual, or they may well feel uncomfortable enough to leave, with the consequent loss to the company of the skills they were recruited for.

Further advice can be sought from the Race Relations Employment Advisory Service, contactable through Jobcentres.

School leavers

There are a number of similarities between school leavers and new graduates, such as lack of work experience, the issue of permanence and the adjustment to working with colleagues who have been with the company longer than the newcomer has been alive! These sections may be read together, although naturally each has points specific to each category.

School leavers have usually had little or no experience of work, having undertaken at most short-term vacation jobs, paper rounds and weekend work. It therefore follows that knowledge of any skills cannot be taken for granted. Although they may have some computer skills, how to use a photocopier or fax and how to file papers may be a mystery to them. School leavers may not be trained to use their initiative (though naturally, some will do so), having been 'spoon-fed' information and instructions.

Some will have visited local employers (perhaps your company), and had brief periods of work experience. The more exposure they have had, the easier they will find it to adjust to work. Ask them about their past work experience, and tailor their subsequent training accordingly.

There are many differences that they will have to adjust to:

- the mixed age ranges of their colleagues (for many 30 is seen as old, and 50+ is positively geriatric!)
- the environment is different; factories, laboratories or offices, etc rather than classrooms
- the longer working day, with fewer breaks and lateness not tolerated (no detention, just the sack!)
- the lack of variety in the work – they can't change subjects after every 40-minute period.

School leavers will often be very nervous and unconfident and they may require prolonged training and intensive counselling to bring them up to standard and allay their fears. They will be unused to the discipline of work and the standards required, so must be taught these. Patience and consideration should be shown and attempts should be made to find out their worries, particularly the shy ones, and put their minds at rest as much as possible.

However, many school leavers are keen to learn about the job and want to get 'stuck straight in'. They may see induction courses as just more schooling and supervisors may have to work hard to keep up their initial interest and enthusiasm. Interesting them in promotion possibilities may help, as may assigning a 'buddy' to them, particularly if the buddy has also left school recently.

Safety training is important too, as young people are particularly vulnerable to accidents through lack of experience. They may play dangerous pranks without realising the risks that their high spirits can cause.

School leavers may require a lot of personal attention and general guidance on non-work matters, such as accommodation if they have had to move home. If they are living away from their parents for the first time, this can require a lot of adjustment and, away from parental control, they may be susceptible to alcohol problems and 'wild' spells. Sports and social clubs are particularly beneficial as they can engage in some of their old hobbies through the company clubs and find new interests. School leavers may also need practical advice on how to handle money, having not had any of their own in such quantities before.

New graduates and college leavers

Sandwich course students will have had a period of work experience (the length depending on the kind of course), usually allied to the degree subject they were studying. Depending on their discipline they may be much more knowledgeable about work than school leavers. Those who took arts or languages may find the transfer to work harder than students who read business studies or vocational subjects, but most students will have had holiday jobs, so are much more likely to know about the world of work. Also, many students travel abroad during the vacations so may well have a broader outlook.

New graduates can be tempted to put too great an emphasis on their own specialisms, because they know them and feel comfortable with them, and may need to be reminded of the inter-departmental links and dependencies. They should be shown the context of the work, and given a thorough knowledge of the organisation and the industry. Many organisations assign a mentor to new graduates, thus helping them to acquire information about the organisation and receive guidance about promotion prospects, etc.

Some graduates will be on trainee programmes, where they are moved around the company at intervals to work in different departments for up to two years, before eventually choosing a specialism. This means that on-the-job training will have to be repeated in each new department so that a good understanding of the job and the standards required are gained. If the sub-culture in different areas is dissimilar, this will require a longer period of adjustment.

Like school leavers, new graduates may be less interested in induction programmes, wanting to undertake 'real work'. Their induction course should include practical opportunities to become involved in the work, particularly if they require training before starting the job. Otherwise, the work will seem very remote from what they think they are there for and motivation will wane.

Much has been written about self-managed learning and new graduates often respond to this particularly well, treating the learning sessions as projects and becoming actively involved in determining their needs, organising their own training and creating support networks. However, other colleagues may feel that they are a privileged group and that *they* were not given what they perceive as special treatment. Self-managed learning and active, participatory induction courses may get them involved and interested, but at the expense of the rest of the job which then seems boring by comparison; balance is required.

It has been noted that many graduates have high expectations of work and the responsibilities they will be given, which are often not borne out by reality. They experience a change of status from university to work. They know that they are intelligent and those with good academic records will be used to being respected. However, they can be seen by employers as less than useful as they know so little about work. They may never have had to write a business letter and most new graduates have only limited opportunities to influence their work.

The academic style of students may also cause initial problems and should be tackled. They may wish to be rigorous where business colleagues are pragmatic. They may appear to lack common sense because of their theoretical outlook. Business students in particular are used to making decisions in hypothetical situations where events and time-scales are collapsed. They often do not realise that they do not initially have the power to make decisions on major issues and that action usually takes a great deal longer than they anticipate. They do not understand the politicking and they may resist teamwork and collaboration after years of being taught not to copy the ideas of others and lonely hours in libraries.

Although they may be used to spending time alone, they no longer have much information on what is required of them (their role is completely changed) and can therefore find it difficult to adjust to isolated jobs.

College leavers may have difficulties in dealing with work time-scales. In the past, everything was transient and they did not expect to spend more than a few years in any of their previous institutions; school and college were relatively short-lived experiences (albeit taking most of their life to date). At work they will meet people who have spent 30 years in the job – longer than they have lived for! This can come as a shock and they may find it difficult to think in terms of permanence.

Hours of work may mean that ways of meeting deadlines are completely different. Office hours are set and staff cannot work for a while, then spend a couple of hours in the local pub before recommencing work on a project, finishing in the early hours of the morning and sleeping all the next day.

As a student the individual can be resilient, ignoring an unsympathetic tutor by either changing courses or putting things into perspective alongside the comments and feedback from other tutors. At work, the boss wields more power and cannot usually be changed.

New graduates will have been used to getting quick and full feedback and are likely to value this in the workplace – not quite marks out of ten, but they do need to know how they are progressing and be given specific pointers and guidance. Expectations should be clear as graduates lack the framework within which to interpret their progress. Targets should not be over-ambitious or adjustment can be more stressful; they are used to succeeding and may fear failure. Failure can produce a vicious circle of passivity, self-doubt and further failure. However, they need challenges and meaningful goals, and these can be built up as the manager sees how the new graduate is progressing.

Building up new job successes helps the new graduates to learn about themselves. They may have had no real idea of their practical skills and capabilities before. All these aspects must be dealt with as part of their induction to work.

Managers and executives

If induction is ineffective for senior managers, the company productivity and image can suffer significantly. It will also have an immediate impact on their own team and direct subordinates.

New senior managers should be welcomed by the top executive and congratulated on their appointment.

Bosses are human; they want to be accepted and share a need for information with other new recruits. Like promotees, they may tend to see the new job in terms of the old one rather than accepting the differences. These links must be weakened so that they can begin to identify more positively with the new job, and give up activities and behaviour that are no longer appropriate.

The new manager needs to know the limits of their own authority and that usually given to their staff. A manager with high acceptance needs may give away too much authority and control early on, making it hard to regain. They should be encouraged to state from the outset that no immediate commitments should be made until they have got to know the work and the team and had time to digest the new information. This may be difficult; their natural instinct may be to make changes, 'marking their territory' to distinguish it from that of predecessors.

New managers and executives should be counselled carefully and allowed to use their initiative (after all, that is what they were employed for) and manage some of their own induction and introductions, etc. They need to find out what they have to do to establish credibility with their boss, their subordinates and the organisation as a whole. Induction should include a detailed breakdown of what is important in the organisation and why, giving them a good understanding of the business and its politics.

Helping them to build the team

In order to help new managers integrate with the organisation and begin to be effective, tactful individual counselling should be given. A mentor, at a similar or higher level, can be assigned to offer advice and guidance. This person should preferably be trained in workplace counselling and giving feedback. They can suggest that the manager answers various questions in order to determine what training needs exist in terms of building the team. Examples of questions that could be talked through include:

- How much do you know about team building?

- What happened when you joined teams in the past?
- What tactics or strategies did you adopt and were they successful?
- If not, what would you like to do differently and how and why do you think that would work?
- How did you feel about building the team and your role as leader?
- What reactions and feedback did you get from the team members?
- Were any surprising issues raised? What and why?
- How can you evaluate your approach to the team and your success as its leader?

Unless the new manager is experienced in team building, they should be given advice and guidance, and specific information such as how much time they are likely to have to meet and build relationships with their new team and how much of their time must be devoted to meeting deadlines and getting the job done.

New bosses should speak to each of their team members individually as well as addressing them as a group. They are likely to feel as nervous as the newcomer, who should disclose their own needs for information and acceptance and persuade the team members to share concerns, fears and expectations. They can be asked what they like and dislike about the job, what barriers exist which hinder performance of the job or completion of the tasks and what their personal goals are. An open manager will ask what they can do to help and what would hinder the work of their subordinates. The manager can usefully ask team members how they prefer to operate (in terms of their jobs) and begin to address issues arising from distribution of the work.

The new manager should ensure that the timing of these meetings does not impair the ability of any of the team to meet deadlines. It is common for the manager to forget that assuming subordinates can drop everything to talk to them can ruin the time management of the individuals concerned. Arrange a mutually convenient time rather than telling subordinates when the meeting(s) will take place. Managers should make notes as it is easy to forget salient points and nuances when bombarded with so much new information. If the subordinate makes a point which the manager acknowledges at the time but then forgets, the person concerned will feel that they have not been listened to or taken seriously. However, in order to build trust, people should be assured that, if notes are taken, nobody else will see them.

New managers should be encouraged to make it clear that, as not everyone is the same, different viewpoints are to be expected and encouraged. They should discuss how these conflicts should be dealt with and who will make the final decision – the manager or the team. These discussions will help to cement the team in its new format.

Some American companies have new manager orientation programmes in which the new manager introduces himself or herself then leaves the staff with a facilitator. The group work to decide what they want to know about the new manager and what they want the new manager to know about them, together with issues they would like to discuss. The latter may include action that the new manager is taking which the group want to continue or stop. The facilitator then meets the manager privately to consider how the matter should be addressed and finally the whole team meets to discuss the issues and solve problems. A follow-up meeting is arranged for about six months later so that progress can be measured.

Establishing the norms

Initial actions taken by the new manager or executive will establish the norms for the group and govern how the team will operate. Norms are sets of assumptions or expectations shared by the team on what kind of behaviour is tolerated or not accepted, or good or bad. Norms can be explicit, like rules, or implicit – more subtle and implied by the mode of behaviour. They are very powerful sets of peer pressure and behavioural controls. If they are violated, the team reacts against them, subtly through silence or glowering looks, etc, or more obviously by cutting remarks and displays of anger.

Norms are often established as a result of critical incidents and the way these are handled. For example, if the manager has their authority challenged by one of their team members, this is an incident. If the manager argues and fights back, and the group supports this either through silence or joining in the rebuke, the norm becomes 'do not challenge the boss'. If, however, the challenge provokes a discussion and team members are encouraged to voice their opinions, open and honest discussions where ideas can be tested or questioned become the norm. If there is conflict between group members and the manager intervenes, conflict can be suppressed as a response to fear of rebuke. If the manager does not get involved, this can either help the team to sort out their own problems, or it can create a *laissez-faire* management attitude with conflict being denied or not resolved, depending on how it is handled.

The manager should also be encouraged to talk to others in the organisation to find out what their team is seen as being good at, and what it does not do so well and what improvement needs other departments perceive. They may also find out about inter-departmental rivalries and how these affect the work.

Expatriates

Expatriate selection and induction is considerably more difficult than the domestic situation. In addition to possessing all the relevant skills including language fluency, the expatriate has to be able to adjust to the different culture and withstand comparative isolation. It has been said that up to 80 per cent of the assignment failures are because of personal adjustment problems rather than lack of technical skills.

Assuming that the organisation has selected an appropriate candidate for a period overseas, arranging a visit to the location before they take the plunge can help them to begin the adjustment earlier. They will be able to get the feel of the place, meet other expatriates and potential colleagues, and find out how their families will adjust – often crucial in helping them to make the adjustment. After all, who can concentrate fully on work if the family is miserable and just itching to get home to familiar surroundings?

Detailed briefing will need to be given on the culture, the history of the country, the geography, politics and economics. Expatriates will need to understand about the religion and traditions of the people if they are not to commit inadvertent blunders which could make their acceptance in the host country difficult. For instance, there may be completely different norms or subtleties in body language and behaviour (such as not showing anger and customs about eating). Old traditions must be respected; an issue of the Australian *Economist* in 1984 cited an example where expatriate employees had chosen a number of bright young people as supervisors. Within a week, they were all found with their throats cut – the expatriates had not realised that age equalled status and they had therefore broken a fundamental 'rule'.

Individual experience of culture shock can be extreme. It is induced by the removal of familiar sights, sounds and activities, such as differences in street signs and newspapers, language, catching a train, making phone calls, etc. Even the simplest activities need thought and planning in a different environment. People can begin to feel lost and doubt their own abilities. Stress may make them begin to think of the local people as odd or stupid so they become alienated from them, and their organisations can be perceived as inadequate, backward and corrupt. Where expatriates have become disillusioned with their new associates and the country, they may offend through indifference and become an embarrassment to the organisation and the home country.

Common symptoms of culture shock include requests for a transfer home and a dissatisfaction with everything in the new country. The home country may be idealised, with the result that expatriates become even more disillusioned on their return as it cannot live up to their inflated expectations. Withdrawal and alcoholism are often associated with maladjustment to an expatriate situation and personal relationships suffer. Proper induction, with attention paid to strategies for coping with stress, can reduce the negative impact of culture shock.

A clear explanation of the personnel policies that apply to the expatriate should be given. They need to understand what salary will be paid and how, whether allowances are given and for what, when home leave is due and can be taken, and the arrangements for payments for flights, etc. It is also important to ensure that feedback is given on their performance and that communications with the home organisation are not impaired. Expatriates need to be kept in touch – the 'grapevine' is unlikely to reach them and often even simple details are not relayed because they are so easily forgotten.

They will also need a full briefing on what conditions will apply on their return and how their career is expected to progress. Assigning a mentor or sponsor to each expatriate is strongly advised in order to help them maintain links with the home country.

Expatriates need help in re-adjusting on returning home. They may experience differences in status. Abroad they were the ambassador for the company; back home they may be just another employee. It is important that their re-introduction is planned and that they have a real job rather than being in a situation where the company is not sure what to do with them. They may also be considered 'out of touch', which comes as a cruel blow after having been sent abroad to broaden their career.

They may also suffer reverse culture shock, a result of idealisation of the home country and difficulty in adjusting to reality, which may include higher taxes (they may have been protected from these while abroad), unfriendliness (people may not be particularly interested in hearing of their experiences overseas), and difficulty in finding employment for other members of the family. Induction, including practical help for the family, can greatly increase the chances of successful re-adjustment for the returning employee, and lessen the chances of financial loss from international ventures for the organisation.

Transferees, promotees and members of project teams

People who have transferred or been promoted within the same company will obviously know all about the organisation and its products and markets, etc, but will need more specific training and guidance on exactly what their job involves, and perhaps new job skills. If the location or department is different, some familiarisation will be involved. The cultures, the 'way we do things around here', may be different, but their general anxiety levels should be lower than for other new starters.

It may be useful for these people to attend part of the formal induction course covering any details that they do not already know, including the initial introductions so that they can get to know their new colleagues. They may be useful examples for induction trainers to point out, proving that promotions do happen.

The probationary period for the job, if any, should be explained thoroughly and it must be made clear what the outcome will be, should their performance not reach the required standards within the specified timescale. If they are dismissed for not reaching the required standards and they have over two years' service, they can claim unfair dismissal if insufficient training was given. Previous service in the organisation, and the fact that they were obviously seen as having potential in order to be promoted, will be taken into account.

Newcomers to project teams may also be neglected in terms of their induction needs although they are new recruits to the group. This is likely to be even more exaggerated if the duration of the project is short. Their integration is important, however, or they can maintain allegiance to their former group. This is especially true if they are to return there at the end of the project and believe that their chances of promotion will come through their former manager rather than the project team leader. In multi-function project groups, members may remain loyal to their function, eg engineering, finance or design, rather than building a primary commitment to the project goals. The group will suffer if no cohesion is created and may revert to simply a collection of people with individual, and often hidden, agendas.

After the organisation's redundancies

If your organisation has made redundancies in the recent past, other staff may well be demotivated which can cause difficulties for new staff. A recruitment freeze may just have been lifted, or the newcomer(s) may be taken on to undertake jobs for which none of the redundant staff was qualified.

The difficulties you encounter may include:

- how to encourage newcomers to stay and make a career with the company
- how to encourage them to be creative and take initiatives when surrounded by others who are suffering from low morale
- how to avoid 'presenteeism' where workers have not actually left, but have 'switched off' and are present in body rather than spirit
- how to run an induction programme with too few staff to do that effectively.

Immediate tasks include providing a support system for the new recruits and finding others in the organisation who can help with their induction. Harnessing the support of the immediate supervisors of the newcomers will be crucial. They should be trained and encouraged to remember back to *their* first days and asked to help draw up an action plan for the newcomers covering the first months. As well as the 'usual' activities of induction, plans should cover the introduction of role models and social events, encouraging newcomers to network with others in a similar position. Support will be vitally important as their demoralised colleagues are unlikely to be able to give them the support they need.

If there are enough new recruits, self-managed learning can be a useful technique to allow them to harness expertise elsewhere in the company without the usual back-up of the personnel or training departments. New employees can be asked to draw up their own training programmes and to arrange talks by the people they want to hear.

Individual development plans should be adopted, provided that budgets to pay for any necessary training can be found. If not, individual plans will only raise false expectations and newcomers are likely to leave.

After the individual's unemployment

If the individual has been unemployed before joining the company, rather than the company having made redundancies, special arrangements should involve extra help to rebuild their confidence and adjust to work again. They may tire easily initially even if keen to work just because they are not used to it, and may worry about the possibility of failure and being unemployed again.

Older workers

Older workers should be respected for their wealth of experience but may find it more difficult to change their working habits than younger colleagues. This may make them lack confidence and induction training should try to bolster this.

Advice for training older workers suggests that training sessions should be extended rather than 'little and often'. Where an older instructor can give job tuition, this will be more acceptable than a 'young whippersnapper' who might make older workers feel intimidated and more worried than ever about failing. Training should be as unlike classroom training as possible. The brightest person in the group should not be used to demonstrate the tasks; pick a slower member of the group so that the fear of failure in the others is lessened. Errors should be pointed out tactfully and encouragement and reassurance given.

Temporary staff

Although it is unlikely that you can justify much expenditure on this group, some induction may be necessary, particularly if they are likely to be with the company for a while, and will therefore be considered by customers as ambassadors for the company in the same way as other staff. If a supplier telephones the organisation, they are unlikely to know that the person they are speaking to is temporary and will expect the usual level of service.

Induction for these people should cover the physical layout of the organisation, some explanation of the interrelationships between departments and the company philosophy for dealing with callers, the public, etc. They will also need knowledge about their immediate area and the duties they are engaged to perform. Although many temporary workers are used to working with little information, it will help them to become efficient more quickly if they have some knowledge of the 'whole picture'.

Giving feedback is an area often neglected with temporary staff, on the basis that if the work is not performed adequately they will be sent back to the agency and a replacement found. If the company values its public image this practice is to be avoided. A little time spent on explaining and perhaps helping them to improve is likely to be rewarded in the way they speak to others about the company.

Points for particular industrial groups

Listed below are some particular aspects applicable to certain industries or areas, which should be included in the induction programme. The list is not exhaustive, but may be a useful prompt list.

- *Agriculture:* chemicals and pesticides, tractors and machinery, milk hygiene and regulations, animal husbandry, hygiene, diseases and deaths, veterinary requirements.
- *Airports:* security and passes, passenger safety and comfort, loss or damage to property, duty free areas and allowances, quarantine regulations, import/export of goods, customs regulations, immigration and emigration, dealing with famous passengers.
- *Banking and finance:* confidentiality of information, handling cash and cheques, etc, FIMBRA.
- *Construction:* site safety (employees, public and operation of equipment), protective clothing, disposal of scrap, theft of property.
- *Computing:* passwords and access to programs, data protection, hacking, computer viruses.
- *Hospitals:* dealing with patients, their families and police, disposal of syringes and equipment, precautions around X-ray areas, precautions against AIDS and hepatitis, drug regulations – care and handling, procedures for dealing with terminal cases and death.
- *Hotel and catering:* dealing with guests and their property, theft, food hygiene, death of guests.
- *Laboratories:* care and transport of dangerous substances, protective clothing, smoking/eating areas, reporting pregnancy if substances likely to harm.
- *Local government:* how to treat the public and the press, officials versus elected members, restrictions on political activities.
- *Manufacturing:* rules on quality standards, hazardous processes and precautions, dangerous/radioactive substances, reporting of breakages, loss of tools, transport of goods.
- *Media:* slander and libel laws, deadlines, advertising, editorial policy and authority.
- *Offices:* style of letters, filing systems, how to answer telephones.
- *Retailing:* customer service policy, rules on store security, customer complaints and staff purchases, uniforms, dealing with bomb threats.

- *Service industries (eg water, gas and electric, etc):* ID cards for entering homes of the public, customer relations and service contracts, safety regulations.
- *Teaching:* dealing with parents, rules on discipline, dealing with truancy, how to handle students' personal problems, needs of the curricula, extra-mural duties, relationships with students.

Chapter 7

Longer-term Needs

Settling in

For induction to be successful, both parties – the employer and employee – need to believe that it will work. Goethe said: 'Treat people as if they were what they ought to be, and you will help them become what they are capable of being.' It will therefore help newcomers if they are encouraged to perform well.

As the newcomers begin to settle in, they go through the questioning period. They will have had time to observe the behaviour of their colleagues, superiors and subordinates and to compare their perceptions of the way their colleagues act with what they have been told about the rules and 'the way things are done around here'. Managers may have to justify unenforced rules and paper policies if the rest of the workforce does not appear to live by them. This can cause disillusionment in the new employee if he or she feels that the rules are right and real life does not quite emulate them. The first flush of enthusiasm could be lost as the newcomers drift into indifference.

The amount of attention the manager needs to give to the newcomer will vary depending on the progress they are making with the job and the acceptance they are gaining from their co-workers. Although they are now settling down, newcomers require continued support as their confidence is brittle and encouragement is still necessary. Networking will augment this and, particularly for graduates, a mentor may be assigned so that they have regular meetings to discuss their development with someone other than their immediate supervisor. When embarking on a mentoring scheme for newcomers, organisations should carefully consider the issues involved. Mentors must be knowledgeable about the company, trained counsellors and avoid taking sides or being drawn into conflicts with the newcomer's superior.

As well as giving continuous feedback, managers should conduct a formal review in private after one month, then again at two months and three months. Discussions should cover progress and performance so far, the likelihood of the employee being retained, and touch on what the future could hold.

To become fully integrated and help the business maintain its efficiency, employees should be encouraged to share their ideas. New recruits can be a rich source of good ideas as they see the work freshly. They may see better ways of doing things than old hands, who perhaps cannot 'see the wood for the trees'. Alternatively, they may just have different experience and expertise which can be used.

If you wish to encourage new ideas it is important not to be critical or to embarrass the person suggesting them. They must not believe that the manager will take all the credit for the idea or that the manager will view the newcomer as a troublemaker because changes have been suggested. If the suggestions are not taken up, the reasons should be properly and thoroughly explained and discussed.

Giving feedback

Research has proved the importance of giving feedback on performance. Improvement is substantially more difficult when the learner does not know how they are doing. This is not only important in the induction phase but also sound management practice throughout employment.

Good managers are 'people growers', enabling subordinates and sometimes colleagues to grow and develop through the tasks set and feedback given. Development of newcomers will not be aided by 'mushroom management' – keeping them in the dark and throwing manure on them! Show new employees recognition by remembering not just their names but a few salient facts about them, such as their interests and hobbies. Newcomers will learn by example (see also Chapter 2), particularly from those closest to them, so try to be a role model.

Managers need to be realistic in their expectations. Plateaux in learning curves and times when progress is slow are normal initially. Remember your first days – were you superwoman/man in your first month? Conversely, expectations should not be too low or new recruits will lose stimulation, becoming bored and frustrated. Two-way feedback is important in setting goals and expectations. Asking the newcomer how they feel and whether they are finding work easy or difficult will help you to set targets appropriately. Questions designed to find out how they are coping can be just an informal 'How's it going?' followed by more specific questions if a potential problem is identified.

Managers should watch for ups and downs in the newcomer's performance and moods, and relate these to what they are doing to try to ascertain the roots of the problem. Part of their responsibility is to try to maintain their motivation, and to keep them trying to improve even where they are having difficulties.

The old adage of praise in public and criticise in private should not be forgotten, though ignoring the former will be less damaging than the latter (for both the employee and the organisation, which engenders fear and loses the respect of everyone by this). Praise can range through the following degrees of detail:

'good job' – pat on the back – post it note – written thanks note – public praise – plaque – performance appraisal

Feedback should be invited where possible and the recipient should at least agree to listen. Unsolicited and unwelcome 'advice' is not helpful. Feedback should be part of a two-way process so the recipient has the opportunity to respond, challenge or explain. Feedback should be specific, constructive, timely and actionable.

Specific feedback means that examples should be cited, eg fault rates, etc, so that it is clear and understandable.

If there are problems, they can be cured by tackling them then and there. Feedback should be quick; it is no use saving up a secret list of wrongs to address the employer with at a three-monthly chat. Note that silence reinforces, so if you do not say anything about their performance, they will assume that it is sufficient, even if it is not.

If performance is good, it needs to be encouraged or it may deteriorate. The employee may think that you had not noticed, or that their performance was not good enough, with subsequent demotivation and deterioration of work.

Feedback should be detailed:

- Explain the situation clearly, giving examples, ie *what* was good or bad, eg not 'you don't listen', but 'you interrupted the client on three occasions when they tried to make a point'.
- Explain why it pleased or displeased you, ie *why* it was particularly good or bad. What special circumstances were there? What barriers?
- Clarify and reinforce the desired result (and perhaps ask them how it could be improved on another occasion).
- Show that you are confident they can attain this result (again), encouraging them to do as well or better in the future.

Showing *why* the performance pleased you is important. A simple 'thank you' is appreciated but is not specific enough to reinforce the action or to give real recognition about why it was good. Employees need to know that you understood the difficulties and barriers they faced in performing the task. If their performance did not please, the reasons must also be clear, so that newcomers understand exactly what you want, what leeway or approximations can be tolerated and why. Asking them to tell you what they are going to do in future, or how they will go about a task, is a useful way of ensuring that they understand.

Feedback must also be fair and balanced. It must not overdo the praise or criticism or the picture they get will be distorted. They will relax too much because they have concentrated on the praise, or worry because the one negative aspect was completely overplayed.

Feedback must be constructive, helping new starters to understand what changes they must make. It must be actionable – only given on elements of performance that can be changed, never on the past which cannot be changed, or on the person's personality. It is not helpful to speculate about the newcomer's motives – stick to *what* they did rather than trying to find out *why*. Feedback should focus on the event rather than the individual, eg not 'you're so stupid' but 'that was not a wise action to take because ...'

Feedback should be personalised, focusing on the impact that the actions had on you, rather than stating it as an absolute truth.

Hurtful criticism will bring changes but without commitment. Even constructive criticism can be damaging, and it has been shown that one piece of negative feedback requires four positive 'strokes' to redress the balance.

Giving feedback should be an ongoing and regular process, with corrections and guidance given at the time, and the formal appraisal process heralding no surprises. The discussion at a formal appraisal stage should summarise what has happened before and give both parties the chance to discuss their expectations and worries for the next period. The whole appraisal procedure should not be just a three-monthly chat, but involve constant monitoring of performance with feedback.

More frequent monitoring and feedback are required in the initial stages than later on in an individual's career. However, support systems should not suddenly disintegrate after the individual has had the induction 'honeymoon period', so that they become isolated and starved of communication. The need for training, coaching and feedback should gradually decrease in frequency to the same levels as for others (where again, they should receive regular monitoring and performance review and no appraisal discussion should come as a surprise).

The induction process can be developed so that the new employee begins to take charge of their own training and learning, and can undertake some self-appraisal.

Formal appraisal

Managers should prepare for the formal appraisal and review as they would for any other interview. Individuals should be given notice of the meeting and time to prepare for it. There should be no interruptions and the manager should try to set them at ease initially.

It may be useful to begin the discussion by asking the newcomer to say how they feel they are progressing, giving a self-assessment. The newcomer can be asked how they see their strengths and weaknesses, what they feel are their main achievements so far and what they enjoy or dislike about the job. Appraisal is a two-way process and requires respect on both sides. In addition to the manager telling them how they are doing, and giving advice and guidance on improvement, the employee must have the opportunity to ask questions and indicate problems, even if this requires consequent improvement or changes in behaviour from the manager! The manager may be unaware of actions which hinder the performance or create difficulties for subordinates. Be ready to accept feedback – keep calm, don't argue (at least until you have heard the whole example), ask for clarification if needed and decide what to do. That could be to discuss the problem, or think about it before deciding how to respond. The newcomer's points should not be ignored any more than yours.

Managers should be able to cite examples which corroborate their judgements. Gathering performance information about the individual will enable the manager to dispel any stereotypes and put first impressions into context. The individual can then be fairly assessed on their merits.

The appraisal discussion should centre on the employee's performance. If the employee raises personal problems, these can be discussed if they are likely to have an impact on the work or are relevant to it. If not, arrange another time to discuss them rather than being sidetracked from the main purpose of the meeting.

At the end of the appraisal discussion the main points should be summarised. The summary should include:

- The newcomer's views of their performance and how they can improve their performance
- Feedback and comments from the manager on the newcomer's progress and achievements
- Ideas for making the job more interesting
- Their aspirations and chances of achieving them
- Their strengths and weaknesses, likes and dislikes
- Any training needs identified
- Training agreed, on or off the job, in-company or external.

The summary should be documented and, preferably, agreed and signed by the jobholder. Examples of appraisal forms are given at the end of the chapter.

Ideally, the subject of pay should be avoided in an appraisal interview as the newcomer may feel (perhaps rightly) that they should not admit weaknesses or their pay increase will not be as good as it would otherwise be. This reluctance to be open and honest is understandable but may affect their performance later if training needs are not identified and acted upon.

Merit pay schemes

Feedback is particularly important where organisations have performance or merit pay systems, to enable the individuals to understand why they achieved the level of pay increase given. The increase should be congruent with the information they have been given or it will cause confusion. If a newcomer (or longer-term employee) is consistently told that they have done an excellent job, well above average, they will expect an above-average rise and are likely to be demotivated if they do not get it. Conversely, if they believe that their performance is adequate but nothing special but they receive a good increase in salary, perhaps similar to those they know are high performers, the incentive to improve and work harder is removed.

Goal setting

In order to have something to appraise people against, it is a good idea to establish goals and targets. Where possible they should be mutually agreed. Elements of goals include:

Specific
Measurable
Attainable
Realistic
Time, with deadline

Setting goals gives them something to aim for; negotiating them ensures that they are achievable and that the individual is committed to them. Measurement and time-scales with milestones add incentives and proof that tasks have been done. Personal goals as well as work activities can be included.

It is important that standards of work are clear, particularly if others in the group are not pulling their weight but have been around longer so are more secure and perhaps more difficult to deal with. The newcomer must not feel victimised – that you are demanding something unfairly from them but not from their colleagues – but must understand that standards are important and that you intend to appraise by them. Show that you are attempting to improve the performance of the less-effective colleagues too.

Help them to get things done by helping them to:

- manage their time
- manage their work
- manage themselves.

Giving instructions

When giving information and feedback, either orally or in writing, use simple everyday language and examples to illustrate your points. The newspaper the employee reads may tell you something about the way in which they expect to receive the written word. Avoid jargon which can be a barrier to understanding and abbreviations which may mean one thing in one area of the company and something else in another.

If instructions are to work properly, they should be clear and concise. Although you should not be patronising, if you assume from the outset that they may have difficulty in understanding you are more likely to take the time to explain the tasks properly and thoroughly. Employees are not clairvoyant and different ways of learning will necessitate different approaches. It has been said that when all other forms of communication fail, try words!

Check that the recipient has understood properly by asking them to explain what they are going to do or how they intend to tackle the task. If the newcomer becomes anxious about what they have to do, they may 'block' the instructions, not hearing them properly. *Listen* to what they tell you to check their understanding and vary the instructions, putting a different slant on them if at first they appear not to respond.

If the task involves a practical skill, tell them how to go about it, then show them and finally watch while they try before leaving them to do it alone. Remember that silence reinforces, so if you watch them getting something wrong, *tell* them, or they will be getting positive feedback.

If instructions are written, ensure that they are clear. Use white space well to break up the points. If a flow diagram can be used for a process, etc this is likely to be much clearer and more easily understood than half a page or so of narrative. Charts can make financial information more user-friendly.

If the duties are complex or involve a number of tasks, it is helpful to outline the expected results and discuss the resources needed to achieve them. Encourage proper planning for complex areas, rather than leaving newcomers under-supervised. Although many people assert that they do their best work under pressure, this makes no allowances for sudden changes and permits procrastination until the last minute. Planning work effectively so that contingencies can be accommodated is more likely to ensure that deadlines are met.

Solicit employees' ideas on how things could be improved and involve them in decision-making where possible, so that you create a more responsive two-way process. The more employees are involved in responsibility for the quality of the product, service or task, the better the result is likely to be. Involving them breeds trust and helps them to take a pride in their work. In the majority of cases, the employer is not looking for blind obedience, rather that employees can take the initiative and spot difficulties in advance.

Further information needs

Once the newcomer's newness begins to wear off, they will have received a lot of basic information about the organisation and the job. Knowledge of the people and the environment should be reasonably complete, and their need will be for further information to supplement what they know about the company, with the main focus on the work – how to perform their job better and at full speed.

Further company information, which they did not need initially and would have swamped them, can now be given. This may include details of consultative arrangements. If there is a staff association, they should be given information about this – who else is in their 'constituency', how to use elected members to put their points across and influence decision-making and how to be elected. Having an avenue through which to make their voice heard will help them to feel involved and accelerate their integration and feeling of belonging in the company. This may also be the time to give them more details of staff benefits such as social clubs and societies.

Make sure that employees are kept informed of changes and developments in the company. A feeling of not knowing what is going on quickly destroys trust. The need to be informed is a vital facet in maintaining relationships. This includes financial information and details of competitors. If individuals are told not only how they are doing, but how the company is doing in comparison with competitors, their sense of belonging is increased as they identify better with the organisation.

Feedback from newcomers should be elicited on what else is needed in terms of information and training. Even if you have attempted to tailor their induction to suit their needs, they will have personal preferences for the way information is communicated to them. Additionally, because everyone forgets some details, the information which is retained or forgotten may differ, so it is wise to check what they remember and what else they need to know.

As nobody can answer the 'what don't you know' question because they don't know, you will have to probe this carefully if you have a sneaking suspicion that they do not really understand something or that some areas are still shrouded in mystery. Don't give them an intensive 'grilling' though, or they will feel threatened and be unlikely to admit that there are grey areas.

Probationary period and potential problems

The probationary period is designed to allow the employer to assess the newcomer's performance and determine whether or not they will become acceptable employees. The employer will need to assess:

- the standard of work – quantity and quality
- personal standards – timekeeping and appearance, etc
- interpersonal or social skills – and ability to mix with other employees
- interest in the job and loyalty to the company.

The length of the induction process should be associated with the length of the learning curve and the time normally taken for individuals doing this type of work to become effective. The probationary period should reflect this, being longer if the job has major pressure points and peaks and troughs throughout the year or needs substantial subjective judgement. However, in many organisations there is a standard three-month, six-month or one-year probationary period for all employees (which should be long enough to cover learning time for all posts).

The individual should understand how long the probationary period is, whether it can be extended and, if so, for what reasons. Some employers favour keeping staff in the dark about this, on the grounds that if new employees feel secure, they will relax their efforts and stop working. The opposite is usually true. Once they feel secure, worries evaporate and they can continue to do well and improve their performance.

The outcome of the probationary period should be monitored by continuous assessment of the individual's performance during the period. The individual should have a formal review at the end of this period. If the review is documented they should be given a copy of this and asked if they have any comments to make.

If all is well their employment should be confirmed. If their performance reaches and sustains acceptable levels before the end of the probationary period, the probation can be terminated early. Despite this, it is as well to check progress after nine months if the probationary period is six, just to ensure that the situation is still satisfactory.

It is normally expected that after about three months (less for manual staff) the newcomer should have settled in and begun to identify with the organisation. Stress can be positive or negative, but by now the effects should have worn off. However, it is easier for some people to adjust than others, and some may develop potential problems which would cause them to leave if not dealt with as they arise.

Danger signals include:

- slow work rate, showing little improvement
- erratic work standards, inconsistent quality
- sudden drop in work quality or standards
- constant errors
- resistance to constructive criticism
- attention seeking
- disruption of the work of others
- touchiness, moods and/or snapping at people
- unpunctuality
- withdrawal, 'presenteeism' or disinterest
- negative attitude
- frequent and/or prolonged absence
- headaches or other minor ailments.

There may be any number of reasons for such problems and it is the manager's responsibility to ascertain the cause, so that appropriate action can be taken. Headaches, minor ailments and absences may be a reaction to stress, either at home or work. The newcomer may not fit in with the rest of the group, may dislike the job or be disappointed by it. They may find the work too easy or too difficult or dislike the company style (whether perceived as too bureaucratic or too chaotic). They may have personal problems but not yet know anyone at work well enough to talk about their difficulties. Insufficient training may have been given.

Naturally, if the cause can be established through discussion, remedies may be found. Even if the problems are personal and outside your control, there may be avenues that can be suggested to help them. If the problem is work-related, because of misunderstandings about the quality or quantity of work, this can be explained, standards clarified and coaching given.

Dismissal

However, if performance does not improve, the subject of dismissal will have to be broached. Proper feedback should ensure that the individual is in no doubt about the seriousness of the position, their shortcomings and the possible outcome. If they are liable to be dismissed they must be told so that they are given an opportunity to improve. Improvement is, of course, the goal. Dismissal and re-recruitment are expensive in both time and money.

If dismissal takes place after the individual has been employed with the company for over two years, they have recourse to an Industrial Tribunal if they feel that they have been unfairly dismissed. If they believe that their dismissal was on the grounds of race, sex or marital status, the two-year qualifying period does not apply. An Industrial Tribunal will need to be convinced that proper feedback, coaching and warnings were given. The statement of dismissal or notice should give the reasons for the termination of employment, referring to earlier feedback and should give details of the particular areas of the job where performance was less than adequate.

If the individual was a promotee these questions will be particularly pertinent and the company should also have considered options for demotion or transfer.

Extension of the probationary period

If the employee's performance has not reached satisfactory standards but is showing signs of improvement, the probation may be extended. This is normally only considered for those not quite good enough, rather than for those whose performance is lacking in a number of areas, or very seriously. The probation should only be extended if the supervisor believes that it is possible for them to reach and maintain acceptable standards. If it looks as if they will never get to that level, they should not be retained. It therefore follows that extending the probationary period is a matter for judgement. The decision should take into account the cost of training, etc and the likelihood of improvement. The cost and time of recruiting another new employee may exceed the cost of the extra training needed to enable the newcomer to perform at an acceptable level. The issues should be discussed openly with the newcomer who should be aware that they will only be retained if performance reaches acceptable levels. They should, however, be given every encouragement to achieve this, along with any necessary further training and individual coaching.

Decisions on extension of probation, the length of the extension and the reasons for it should be recorded in writing and a letter to this effect should be given to the employee. The letter should inform them that if they reach the required standard they will become permanent members of staff, but if not they will be liable to be dismissed. It should also give details of further monitoring which will take place during the extension period and how to appeal against this decision.

Career planning

If the individual and the organisation are happy with each other, thoughts will turn to what comes next.

A survey of 200 North American workers showed that what they wanted was the opposite of what their immediate managers thought they wanted! Table 7.1 shows the importance that managers and their staff gave each of the following:

Table 7.1 *Staff and managers' perceptions of motivating factors at work*

Managers' ranking		Employees' ranking
1	Money	5
2	Job security	4
3	Promotion	7
4	Working conditions	9
5	Interesting work	6
6	Loyalty from the company	8
7	Tactful discipline	10
8	Appreciation	1
9	Sympathetic help on personal problems	3
10	Feeling of being involved	2

The order in which they are listed shows the order in which they were ranked by immediate superiors. It therefore follows that it is unwise to assume that you know what the employee wants – better to ask and plan accordingly.

Discussions about the future can cover promotion prospects and transfers. The newcomer's potential, as diagnosed from the current performance, can be considered, together with aspirations and personal preferences.

Discussions about the future should cover what further training and development are needed for their current post or promotion. This may include informal training, short courses or examination studies with time off and fees paid, depending on needs and company resources. Although you may be constrained by less than generous training budgets, it should be possible to tailor the work to some extent to enable the employee to gain the experience wanted.

Development on the job may be given through projects or special assignments, etc. Work can be planned so that a broad range of duties is undertaken or specialisation in a particular area, according to the employee's wishes and company needs (which are inevitably put first).

Organisations differ in the way that they act upon individual aspirations. In some companies formal career planning may be undertaken involving the immediate manager and their boss and possibly a mentor. In other organisations the individual may be left to work out their own plans and goals and to try to ensure that they are given the experience they need to achieve them.

In large organisations it will probably be necessary to involve higher management in the career planning process, as they are more likely to know what posts and opportunities may be available in the future and where the business as a whole is heading. If commitments cannot be made, they should not be given. Broken promises destroy morale.

Checklist for longer-term needs

1. Are you still giving the newcomer enough support, encouragement, guidance and feedback?
2. Have you undertaken formal performance reviews at regular or monthly intervals? Did you invite the views of the newcomer?
3. Does the newcomer understand the purpose of the probationary period and the outcome of it? Has this been documented?
4. Have you seen any 'danger signals' in their performance or conduct and spoken to them about the problems?
5. Are you benefiting from having 'new blood' and encouraging new ideas?
6. Is your feedback invited, fair, specific, constructive, timely, actionable and personalised? Have you focused on the event rather than the person?
7. Are your instructions clear?
8. Are the goals set specific, measurable, attainable and realistic with agreed deadlines?
9. Have you augmented earlier induction training with further information about the job or the company?
10. Have you assigned a mentor to the newcomer?
11. Has the newcomer been given a realistic idea of their progress in the company, to help shape and temper their aspirations and plan their career?

7.1 End of probation review form and notes for guidance

CONFIDENTIAL

To be completed in black ink

Name of employee________________________________

Job title__________________ Grade__________________

Starting date____________ Date of appraisal interview____________

Probation ends______________ Department______________

To be completed by the immediate supervisor

Please read the associated notes for guidance before completion of this form. Give comments on all the main aspects of job performance, indicating whether the employee is satisfactory or not on each element. Please give examples.

1. Knowledge/expertise
2. Quality of work
3. Quantity of work
4. Results and achievements
5. Interpersonal skills
6. Interest in work
7. Written communications
8. Oral communications
9. Numerical/data skills
10. Conduct and punctuality

11. Staff management

12. Other skills/qualities

Additional comments, overall assessment and training needs:

RECOMMENDATION

A SATISFACTORY	Continue employment
B NOT QUITE GOOD ENOUGH	Extend probation until _____
C UNSATISFACTORY	Terminate employment

Signed______________________________ Date______________________________

Name (print)__________________________ Grade__________________________

Employee's comments:

Employee's signature___________________________ Date_______________

____

Notes for guidance on end of probation form

The form should be completed by the immediate supervisor after discussion with any other managers who have knowledge of the individual's performance. The form should be completed after the appraisal interview and the individual given the option to comment within two weeks.

Categories asterisked should be completed for all employees, other categories as required.

Marking
Employees should be marked A, B or C on each category, where

A = Satisfactory, above required standard
B = Not quite good enough
C = Unsatisfactory, does not meet required standards

Notes on categories:
These are not comprehensive but give an indication of the areas to be appraised.

1.* *Knowledge/expertise*
Knowledge of the job and of the company, technical competence required

2.* *Quality of work*
Accuracy and thoroughness of work, error or fault rates, ability to plan and organise work, judgement, creativity, initiative, ability to work without supervision

3.* *Quantity of work*
Ability to meet deadlines, speed of work, etc

4.* *Results and achievements*
Targets set and achieved, achievements beyond the normal scope of the job

5.* *Interpersonal skills*
Internal: Relationships with other departments, ability to mix with colleagues and peers, attitude to bosses and subordinates, use of tact and diplomacy
External: Relationships with clients/customers and suppliers
General: Persuasion or negotiating skills and assertiveness

6.* *Interest in work*
Attitude, adaptability, drive to improve

7. *Written communications*
Clarity, comprehensiveness, breadth/depth of analysis, brevity and style

8. *Oral communications*
Clear instructions and expressions, understandable

9. *Numerical/data skills*
Computer literacy, proficiency with particular software, accuracy of statistics, etc

10. *Conduct and punctuality*
    Attendance, punctuality, care of equipment, safety consciousness
11. *Staff management*
    Level of supervision, clarity and timeliness of feedback, ability to coach staff, handling discipline
12. *Other skills/qualities*
    Other skills or abilities necessary for the job, eg appearance, determination, etc

Additional comments, overall assessment and training needs
Include any other comments, such as ability to work under pressure, taking on extra work, etc and any further training requirements.

Comments should indicate the reasons for rating A, B or C in the recommendations below.

Full explanations are required in the case of B or C markings and individuals should have been counselled previously on the likelihood of this outcome. Further documentation may be required later. These cases should also be discussed with the personnel department.

Recommendations
A Satisfactory – employment will be continued, contract issued and the staff member will be considered permanent
B Not quite good enough – employment will be extended for a further period during which performance will be kept under continuous review. The recommended duration of the extension of the probationary period should be specified.
C Unsatisfactory – employment will be terminated. The individual will be dismissed.

Employee's comments. Please ensure that the employee has the opportunity to add any comments once the appraisal form has been written. The employee should sign to signify that the form has been read and the contents agreed.

7.2 Letter confirming employment

On letterheaded paper

(Name)
(Address)

(Date)

Dear

I am pleased to inform you that you have successfully completed your three-month probationary period and that your employment as (job title)   with us has now been confirmed.

(Optional paragraph)
As discussed at the appraisal interview, you will need to concentrate on the following areas in the next few weeks:

1. ....
2. ....

If you need any more help on these, please do not hesitate to ask.

I am very pleased to be able to welcome you officially and wish you a long and successful career with us.

Yours sincerely,

(Name)
(Title)

7.3 Letter extending the probationary period

On letterheaded paper

(Name)
(Address)

(Date)

Dear

As you will know from the appraisal discussion with your manager, we are unable to confirm your continued employment with us at present.

The standards of performance required have been explained to you but your performance in the post so far has not matched these. However, in view of the fact that your performance was only slightly short of the acceptable standard, we have agreed to extend your probationary period until (date) to enable further assessment.

I attach a copy of your appraisal report from which you can see that improvement is required in the following areas:

1. ....
2. ....

Your performance will be closely monitored during the extended probation period and you will be given further training and encouragement to help you reach the required standards. However, if your performance is still not adequate by the end of this period, your employment with us will be terminated. Should this happen you will be advised before the decision is taken.

If you would like to discuss this further or you would like any further advice and guidance, please do not hesitate to contact me.

I hope that you will be able to make the necessary improvements and that your continued employment can then be confirmed.

Yours sincerely,

(Name)
(Title)

7.4 Dismissal letter

On letterheaded paper

(Name)
(Address)

(Date)

Dear

I regret to inform you that I am writing to confirm that we have decided not take up your contract and continue your employment with us.

Although I know that you will be disappointed by this, you have been kept informed of the situation and counselled on the areas of your performance which did not meet the standards required.

This letter serves to give you the official statutory notice period of one week and you will therefore leave the company on (date).

Your P45 and final pay cheque will be forwarded to your home address. Would you please arrange to pass any company property you hold to your manager on your last day.

I am very sorry that this particular appointment has not worked out but wish you every success in securing a suitable position shortly.

Yours sincerely,

(Name)
(Title)

7.5 Appraisal record form and notes for guidance

CONFIDENTIAL

Name____

Job title____________________ Date appointed____________________

Date of appraisal interview____________ Appraisal period____________

REFER TO NOTES FOR GUIDANCE BEFORE COMPLETION OF THE FORM. The list below is neither exhaustive nor definitive. You do not have to complete every section and other aspects may be added if these are relevant.

1. Duties
   Is the job description still accurate? Yes/No
   If not, please attach a new job description and outline the major responsibilities below.

   ____

   ____

2. Targets and objectives

Targets set	Achievements against targets

	Marking
3. Knowledge/expertise	☐
4. Quality of work	☐
5. Quantity of work	☐
6. Interpersonal skills	☐
7. Interest in work	☐
8. Written communications	☐
9. Oral communications	☐
10. Numerical/data skills	☐
11. Conduct and punctuality	☐
12. Staff management	☐
13. Other skills/qualities	☐

General comments and overall assessment

OVERALL MARKING

☐	A	VERY GOOD PERFORMANCE
☐	B	SATISFACTORY
☐	C	NOT QUITE GOOD ENOUGH
☐	D	UNSATISFACTORY

Training needs

The future

Please sign and date this record of the appraisal.

Signed________________________ Date________________________

Name (print)______________________ Grade________________________

TO BE COMPLETED BY THE EMPLOYEE:

Please complete as appropriate

A I agree that the information given here represents a true record of the appraisal interview and discussion.

Employee's signature____________________ Date____________________

Comments I wish to add:

B I disagree with aspects of this record and discussion. I would like to make the following amendments/I attach the following explanation.

Employee's signature____________________ Date____________________

Notes for guidance on the appraisal form

The form should be completed by the immediate supervisor after the interview and prior discussion with any other managers who have knowledge of the individual's performance. The individual should be given the option to comments within two weeks.
Categories asterisked should be completed for all employees, others as applicable.

Marking
Employees should be marked A, B, C or D on each category, where

A = Very good performance, well above average
B = Satisfactory, at or above required standard
C = Not quite good enough, training needs identified, performance to be kept under review
D = Unsatisfactory, does not meet required standards, will require warning about performance

Notes on categories:
Examples *must* be given to illustrate the points/markings.

1.* *Duties*
Please give details of changes in responsibilities
2.* *Objectives/targets*
Note objectives set together with performance against them. If targets have not been met, give reasons
3.* *Knowledge/expertise*
Knowledge of the job and of the company, technical competence required
4.* *Quality of work*
Accuracy and thoroughness of work, error or fault rates, ability to plan and organise work, judgement, creativity, initiative, ability to work without supervision
5.* *Quantity of work*
Ability to meet deadlines, speed of work, etc
6.* *Interpersonal skills*
Internal: Relationships with other departments, ability to mix with colleagues and peers, attitude to bosses and subordinates, use of tact and diplomacy
External: Relationships with clients/customers and suppliers
General: Persuasion or negotiating skills and assertiveness
7.* *Interest in work*
Attitude, adaptability, drive to improve
8. *Written communications*
Clarity, comprehensiveness, breadth/depth of analysis, brevity and appropriateness of style

9. *Oral communications*
   Clear instructions and expressions, understandable
10. *Numerical/data skills*
    Computer literacy, proficiency with particular software, accuracy of statistics, etc
11. *Conduct and punctuality*
    Attendance, punctuality, care of equipment, safety consciousness
12. *Staff management*
    Level of supervision, clarity and timeliness of feedback, ability to coach staff, handling discipline
13. *Other skills/qualities*
    Add notes on any other skills or abilities necessary for the job, eg appearance, determination, ability to work under pressure. Show how the individual meets these.

General comments and overall assessment
General comments can include broad strengths and weaknesses and any particular points raised by the appraisee.

Overall marking
The overall marking follows the same scheme as that shown above. Comments should indicate the reasons for rating A, B, C or D.
Full explanations are required in the case of C or D markings and individuals should have been counselled about the outcome of this if no improvement is shown.

Training needs
Record any recommendations for training, in-company or external courses or on-the-job help. Recommendations should cover training for improving job performance before future prospects. Any help the appraiser can give to enable the appraisee to improve should also be noted.

The future
Discuss, agree and itemise specific objectives/targets or plans for the next year. Note any development action needed to help the appraisee develop their career.

Employee's comments. Please ensure that the employee has the opportunity to add any comments once the appraisal form has been written. The employee should sign to signify that the form has been read and the contents agreed.

7.6 Notes for guidance for those undergoing appraisal

The work and development of (company name) depends to a large extent on the competence and effectiveness of its staff. We therefore need to know about your performance, potential and personal wishes. The object of appraisal is to help improve the individual's performance, to give them feedback on how they are doing, to help them realise their potential and achieve better results for the company.

It is (company name)'s policy that people should be appraised every (interval of appraisal, eg six months, one year). It is intended that the appraisal interview should facilitate a two-way flow of information and communication.

The interview will enable discussion on your performance and subsequent documentation of this. It is not intended as a forum for releasing stored grumbles and groans which could have been raised earlier. It is not an interview for promotion or for a salary increase.

Notice

You should be given (time, eg one week, 48 hours, etc)'s notice of the appraisal interview which should be held in a quiet place where your conversation will not be disturbed or interrupted.

Prepare for the interview

The interview will be most constructive if you are prepared for it. Think about the points you wish to raise, your strengths and weaknesses and any difficulties you have. Check your job description before the interview to ensure that it is still accurate.

The value of the appraisal will depend largely upon what you contribute to it. Your appraiser should provide examples to illustrate why he/she feels that your performance deserves the marking discussed. You should be prepared to discuss ideas (your own and those suggested to you) about your job, your performance of it, your training requirements and your future. You are not required to discuss any subject with your appraiser which is personal and not related to your job.

You may wish to make notes to take to the interview with you. Do this if it helps you remember the points you want to raise.

Questions to think about before the interview

1. *Your job*

(a) Do you understand all the aspects of your job?

(b) Does your job description match what you actually do or take responsibility for?
(c) Does your job overlap with anyone else's?
(d) Do you feel that you are given the right level of responsibility?
(e) Are the targets fair and priorities clear?
(f) Do you have any constructive suggestions which would make your job more interesting?

2. *Your performance*

(a) How well do you think you do your job? (Why? Give examples.)
(b) What do you consider to be your strengths/development areas in this job? (Why? Give examples.)
(c) What do you enjoy most/least?

3. *Barriers to performance*

(a) How could you improve your performance?
(b) What are the barriers to improving your performance, or which prevent or restrict you from performing your job effectively?
(c) Do you feel that communication with others is adequate?

4. *Your training needs*

(a) Are there any areas where you feel that additional information, help or training are needed?
(b) Specifically, what assistance do you need?
(c) Are you up-to-date with the latest developments in your specialism?
(d) Is there anything that would help you and also benefit the company?

5. *Grouses*

(a) Are there any minor changes in your immediate environment which would make a difference?
(b) Is there anything that really irritates you that could easily be improved? (NB This is designed to elicit problems the organisation can do something about, not the local bus times, etc.)

6. *Your future*

(a) In which direction do you hope to progress? When?
(b) What extra training or experience do you think you need to prepare yourself for your next career move?

After the interview

Shortly after the interview, your manager should write up the record of your discussion. The record should be accurate but does not need to reproduce every detail – just the salient points.

You will be asked to sign a copy to show your agreement. If you cannot agree, you should arrange another meeting to discuss points of dissent. If you still do not agree, record your own account in the space on the form. You may also wish to speak to your boss's boss about this.

Chapter 8

Evaluation of Induction

The Institute of Personnel Management has reported that few companies evaluate their induction programmes. Many do so as a response to a perceived problem, such as a higher than expected number of leavers, rather than undertaking the exercise for its own merits. However, the benefits of doing so are apparent – to ensure that the company is spending its money effectively and that the methods of helping new employees to integrate and become effective quickly are working.

Evaluation can cover many aspects and be done at various levels, depending on the complexity of the programme and the resources available. There are a number of quantitative measures, data that may well be collected by the organisation anyway, such as labour turnover statistics, accident rates, sickness and absenteeism rates, etc. Qualitative information has to be gathered separately through questionnaires and surveys, exit interviews and course evaluation forms. This evidence is important but more difficult to collect as it relies on the interpretation of the newcomers' perceptions, as reported by them.

Before beginning evaluation the company will need to decide which aspects they wish to monitor, who will be involved in the evaluation, and against what time-scales it should be measured.

Who should be involved?

This will depend to some extent on other factors, such as the information to be collected. It will usually involve the personnel department but may not include the line manager in some instances if this is necessary to ensure confidentiality. For instance, exit interviews are often conducted by personnel staff rather than the line manager so that information about the manager and the style of management can be elicited, in case this is pertinent. Thus responses can be collected from the newcomers themselves, at various stages, from the line managers (giving their view on how it has gone), and from mentors and buddies, etc.

In many instances it is likely that confidentiality will have to be assured. In cases where data can only be collected from the newcomers and it is their perceptions that count, they are unlikely to volunteer unfavourable information if it will be divulged. Senior managers may insist on seeing data; in such cases they should be given data on the group rather than anything identifiable on individuals. Senior management involvement is desirable, however, in terms of their interest in the results and commitment to help people become effective quickly. They will also be able to authorise appropriate budgets to enable this to happen.

In order to demonstrate impartiality, it may be useful to bring in external consultants, who will ensure the secrecy of data, to undertake the evaluation. However, if this kind of measure is necessary it probably indicates a high level of distrust in the company.

Time-scales for evaluation

Different elements will need to be measured over different time-scales. An evaluation of the induction course can be undertaken immediately afterwards through the use of course questionnaires. Measuring the difference in labour turnover and the number of early leavers will take substantially longer, as a reasonable time must elapse for the new recruits to complete the induction and before the number who stay with the company for longer than a year can be measured.

Quantitative measures

Quantitative measures are indicators – they may show a problem but further investigation will be needed to identify the cause. Comparisons made are with past data rather than controls so the analyst must ensure as far as possible that other material factors are taken into account.

The average figures should be calculated. The company must then decide how high above the average the measurement has to be before action is taken.

Labour turnover

Labour turnover is usually measured as the number of employees leaving in a specified period, divided by the total number of employees in that period. It is usually expressed as a percentage. Where the number of employees was not constant in the period, the average number of employees is used.

Another associated measure is the employee survival index, giving figures on how long employees stay with the company. Again, this is expressed as a percentage of the total workforce, eg 20 per cent of the workforce have been with the company for longer than two years, etc.

If induction is working well the labour turnover figures should drop after its introduction and the employee survival index should rise. However, it may take a number of years to collect all the evidence so other measures may have to be used. There may also be other influencing factors which should be borne in mind when looking at the statistics.

If turnover statistics are analysed by department, problem areas may be highlighted. This may have more to do with the management of that unit or with job design than induction. It is important to look at all the possible causes.

Sickness and absenteeism

Statistics on sickness and absenteeism may also be routinely collected, and as with labour turnover a rise may indicate poor induction or a number of other factors. It will be useful to compare the average absenteeism for newcomers with the average for 'old hands' to see if a problem is indicated.

It is generally not useful to compare sickness rates of individuals as these will naturally vary between people anyway. An individual with a higher than average sickness rate may be experiencing a sickness rate normal for them; it is up to the organisation to determine whether this is true or whether it represents malingering. The organisation will need to decide what level of absenteeism it will tolerate.

The type of sick leave – amount and frequency – is also an indicator. Those who take odd days off work are more likely to be unhappy at work or suffering from stress than those who are away for longer, where the illness is verified by a doctor's certificate.

If absence follows accidents at work, there may well be a need for better job training. If sickness is high in a newcomer exhibiting other signs of problems, such as being withdrawn or disinterested, it may be due to stress and/or the fact that they have not integrated properly in the organisation.

Accident and fault rates

Similarly, accident and fault rates for newcomers should be compared with the longer serving staff. It is well known that newcomers tend to have higher accident rates, which can be measured in terms of frequency of accidents or severity, or both. High accident rates may indicate a need for better job or safety training or better equipment or safety arrangements.

It is almost inevitable that the fault rates for newcomers will be higher than for long-term employees, because they do not know the job as well. Fault rates are important – they represent money to the company. Statistics on reworking and wastage should also be collected as these indicate errors. The cost of poor quality includes the cost of reworking, wastage and the opportunity costs; for instance, the newcomer could have been undertaking other work rather than the repairs needed.

If the rate remains unreasonably high further job training may be indicated. It is always useful to ask the individuals affected how they think that accidents could be avoided and risks minimised. With high fault or error rates, individuals may be exhibiting presenteeism, being present in body while their minds wander.

Other factual measures

Othe factual measures include:

- Has the induction programme been undertaken by all new employees within the stated time-scales (as specified in the induction policy)?
- Are supervisors using their checklists so that all the information is covered?
- Have buddies and/or mentors been assigned?
- Are log books being completed for all new employees?

Although evidence may show that induction checklists are being used, training may not be uniform. The approach or the way information is conveyed may vary.

Good induction may be indicated by high pay rises after the initial or probationary period, demonstrating that new employees are performing well.

Qualitative measures

Qualitative measures are only as good as the interpretation of the data, which is seldom standard. There are no control groups and comparisons are not direct, like with like, but rely on judgement. However, trends may emerge and norms may well be established, eg a company is likely to know the normal learning time for undertaking a certain type of work.

Appraisals

Evidence taken from appraisals can show whether or not a new employee is performing at an acceptable standard and whether their progress is faster than average. The length of the learning curve can be inferred, but data from a number of individuals will have to be compared in order to be meaningful. After good induction the organisation may notice a reduction in the length of time taken for employees to become fully effective. Changes in recruitment practice may also influence this if better testing means that those with greater aptitude for the job are selected.

Appraisals may give indications of how easy or difficult the individual found the induction and integration and which factors helped or hindered. Appraisal information can be difficult to collect as it is unstructured in terms of the need to monitor induction, having been designed for a different purpose.

Surveys and questionnaires

Surveys can be undertaken by using questionnaires or by interviewing individuals, perhaps using a list of structured questions rather than leaving the discussion completely open, which is harder to analyse and may not collect comparable information.

Questionnaires circulated to newcomers who have undergone the induction programme can be kept anonymous in an attempt to persuade the respondents to reply truthfully. If follow-up is likely, respondents should be asked to give their names. If large numbers are involved, they may be given a choice of giving their name or remaining anonymous providing that enough people will come forward.

The following questions can be asked at the end of an employee's probation or after about six months in order to obtain some feedback on the induction process.

(a) What did you think was useful about the induction process?
(b) What did you like and dislike about the process?
(c) Is there any information that you now have but would have liked earlier?
(d) Is there anything that you are still not clear about?
(e) Do you feel that the job has lived up to your initial expectations? If not, why not?

These can be followed by specific questions for particular areas, eg to see if they feel that they understand the company information and know enough about the products. Although this information is a matter of opinion, these are opinions that count. They show the effect of the induction and whether the individual feels comfortable, a material factor if the organisation wishes them to stay.

Questionnaires and surveys have the advantage of being controllable, ie the questions can be repeated to different groups so that, apart from time, other elements are broadly similar, making comparisons easier.

Evidence can be collected from a wide range of people:

- the newcomers – to ascertain their view, which is of central importance
- their managers – to get an idea of what their performance is really like and how they compare to other new recruits
- mentors and buddies – to find out their perceptions of whether the induction programme is working as it should.

If problems are suspected, questionnaires or surveys can be used to test for them.

Providing feedback on the results of any survey will increase the chance of gaining co-operation for other surveys. People are always interested in the results if they have been sufficiently motivated to take part. They want to believe that their ideas and suggestions have been acted upon. It is also useful to send a separate thank-you letter if their information has been particularly valuable.

Exit interviews

The purpose of the exit interview is to find out why the individual is leaving. This may uncover information about inadequate induction or a host of other problems, or none at all. If there is a problem which can be traced to inadequate induction, the company will want to find out what should (in the employee's view) have been done differently to persuade them not to leave and what changes they would recommend.

Exit interviews are usually conducted by personnel staff who are seen as independent from line management. They can be undertaken as soon as the individual has given in their notice or just before they leave.

The interview must be handled sensitively in order to elicit any useful information. The leaver has no vested interest in co-operating and may worry about the effect of their remarks on the remainder of their notice period, particularly if they think that comments will find their way back to their immediate superior. It is normal to allay their fears by assuring them of confidentiality and promising that the interview will not prejudice their references.

Exit interviews can be a useful source of information even if the person leaving has been with the company some time. Problems highlighted may stem from the induction period.

Although personnel staff may feel that the exit interviews produce worthwhile information, the line managers may think that personnel are just listening to leavers' unjustified grouses and complaints. If there have been any personality problems, they may worry about being blamed for losing a staff member and that their role will be misrepresented by this maverick employee. They may feel that the company is better off without the leaver and that the personnel department is taking sides or reporting to the senior managers.

Evidence from exit interviews may highlight management problems which can be difficult to tackle as confidentiality was promised, but at the same time the person who has collected the evidence will need to do something about the problem. Mechanisms for dealing with this can be developed and senior managers appraised of pertinent information covering the whole group. This requires sensitive handling on all sides.

Some organisations send a questionnaire a short while after the individual has left so that the ex-employee can be assured that references, etc will not be affected and because firms believe that the data collected may be more truthful. However, the number of responses can be very low.

Induction course evaluation forms

It is usual to distribute course evaluation forms at the end of a training period or course. Depending on the course content these can be given immediately after the course, or some time later if it is likely that the material covered will take longer to assimilate or put into context.

Forms usually ask course delegates what they found most and least useful about the course, which parts could have been omitted and which elements they would have liked more time for. They may also be asked to comment on the teaching or speaking style of the presenters and on training aids.

It is important that these forms are not just buried after collection, and that the course is amended in line with comments made. If individuals believe that their views will be taken into account and that the course will be modified along the lines they suggest, they are more likely to put some thought and effort into their contribution.

In addition to asking delegates for their views on the course, it is useful to ask personnel staff or the people who ran the course, if different, for their views. They can say what they think was well received and what was not so successful. They may be able to spot areas where the newcomers may have misunderstood or not really grasped the whole picture.

It will be useful if there is a central co-ordinator for the design and evaluation of induction programmes – ownership helps to ensure that this aspect is not forgotten. The co-ordinator should be from the personnel or training department and should have enough power to ensure that changes can be made and budgets increased. They should also have the interpersonal skills to counsel senior managers or other speakers if their input to the course was found lacking. They may have to coach them in presentation techniques or explain why they intend to choose other presenters in future.

Evaluation of on-the-job induction

It is important that supervisors give feedback on how useful they find their checklists and whether the training they received adequately prepared them to induct the newcomers properly. They can contribute by demonstrating gaps in knowledge where they felt poorly equipped to help the newcomers. If supervisors meet as a group they can work together to find better ways of explaining tasks and/or showing individuals how to operate equipment, etc.

They can give feedback on whether the newcomers appeared to become effective more quickly under the methods they used and can also highlight any areas where the formal induction course did not match what newcomers found at the workplace.

Effective evaluation

The organisation will have to decide the most effective way of evaluating the induction and over what time-scales, taking into account its own needs and any special factors pertaining to them. It is unlikely that any one method will be sufficient; effective evaluation is likely to require assessment of several of the measures above.

If the organisation has planned wisely evaluation will show that induction is effective, and that recruits perform well within a reasonable period. Thus, newcomers are properly integrated, the performance of the company is improving – induction has been successful.

Evaluation checklist

1. Is induction being undertaken by all new employees within prescribed time-scales?
2. Is evaluation of induction being carried out? Does this cover the entire process or just the formal induction course?
3. Does evaluation cover some of the following quantitative measures:
   Labour turnover statistics
   Sickness/absence rates
   Accident rates
   Fault and error rates and wastage?
4. Does evaluation involve the interpretation of information collected from:
   Appraisals
   Questionnaires and surveys
   Exit interviews
   Induction course evaluation forms
   Feedback from supervisors?
5. Does the evaluator have the power to make changes to induction?
6. Are supervisors trained and are they using their checklists?
7. Are log books being completed for new starters?

8.1 Induction course evaluation form

Name of course____________________ Date of course__________

Location____________________ Trainer____________________

Name of course member (optional)____________________________

---

1. Do you consider that the training objectives were met? Yes/No
2. Did you achieve your own objectives? Yes/No
3. Which topic(s) did you find most useful? Why? Could they have been expanded?

   ____

   ____

4. How will you apply them in your present post?

   ____

   ____

5. Which topic(s) did you find least useful? Why? Could they have been eliminated?

   ____

   ____

6. What, if anything, would you like added to the course syllabus?

   ____

   ____

7. Did you consider that information was presented in a useful format? Yes/No
8. Would you have preferred a different ratio of teaching methods? (ie more discussion groups and fewer lectures, etc) Yes/No

If yes, please say what and why.

____

____

9. Was the style of facilitation satisfactory? Yes/No
   If not, why not?

____

____

10. Please tick the boxes below as appropriate to indicate your views on the effectiveness of the speakers and on the topics specified.

    5 = very good
    4 = good – minor points of detail could be improved
    3 = average
    2 = barely satisfactory, room for considerable improvement
    1 = weak

Effectiveness of the speakers:	1	2	3	4	5
Name______________					
Name______________					
Name______________					
Name______________					
Name______________					

	1	2	3	4	5
Pre-course documentation______________					
Administrative arrangements______________					
Supporting paperwork______________					
Visual aids______________					
Accommodation and food______________					

Comments
Please add any comments you may have on the course in the space below.

Thank you for completing this questionnaire.

8.2 Induction log book

Name____________________ Date joined__________

Department____________________ Supervisor__________

Topic	Training completed (date)	Supervisor's initials	Follow-up required
1.			
2.			
3.			

This sheet can be used to cover all the job training required or a separate sheet can be used for each topic.

Examples of topics for induction log book

1. Provide sales invoice manual and explain the main points
2. Explain procedures for:
   - writing invoices and credit check
   - payments by cheque or credit card
   - giving customer discounts
3. Explain use of till
4. Explain cash-handling procedures and security
5. Explain philosophy re: customer relationships and how to deal with complaints
6. Explain Trade Descriptions and Sale of Goods Acts
7. Explain policy re: sale of tobacco and alcohol

8.3 Questions for use in structured exit interviews

The job and working conditions

1. What did you like most/least about your job?
2. Was the job described fairly when you were recruited?
3. How did you feel about your workload?
4. Were your responsibilities and targets clear?
5. (a) Did you receive any training?
   (b) What was it?
   (c) What was your opinion of its usefulness?
   (d) Was there any other training that you think would have been more useful?
6. What did you think about the promotion prospects (and yours in particular)?
7. What was your opinion of the physical working conditions?
8. a) Do you have any suggestions for the improvement of the job or the working conditions?
   b) Have you made these suggestions before?

Relationships

9. What were your relationships like with colleagues/bosses/subordinates? (Try to get examples.)
10. What was morale like in your department?
11. What was your supervisor like?
    (Aim to elicit comments on the amount and appropriateness of praise and encouragement, criticism and feedback, how complaints were handled, whether this individual was dealt with differently, etc.)

Pay and benefits

12. Were you satisfied with the pay and benefits? If not, why not?
13. How did you feel about the holidays, sickness pay, pension scheme, etc. Did you think they were good, average or poor compared to other employers?
14. Are there any other things that you wish to comment on?
15. Were you proud to work for this company?
16. Would you recommend this company to others? If not, why not?

Chapter 9

Further Reading and Information

Further reading

A few books and articles which expand on some areas of this book are listed below. The list is not intended to be a full bibliography, but highlights some useful texts on particular areas of interest.

1. George, R. Thomas (1986) First impressions: how they affect long-term performance *Supervisory Management* (USA) 31 3 : 2–8
2. Linstead, Steve (1985) Organisational induction: the re-creation of order and the re-reading of discourse *Personnel Review* 14 1 : 3–11
3. Handy, Charles B (1986) *Understanding Organisations* Penguin Books, 3rd edn.

The first two articles cover what I have called the behavioural contract and its sociological perspectives. Number 3 is a well-known book packed with readable information on organisational behaviour including culture and how it is formed and the formation and functioning of groups.

4. Lewis, David (1990) *Essentials of Employment Law* Institute of Personnel Management, 3rd edn.

Covering all the major aspects of employment law, this gives a good guide to contracts of employment.

5. Harrison, Rosemary (1988) *Training and Development* Institute of Personnel Management

A must for everyone putting together a training course. This explains some learning theory but is mainly a practical guide to training and development, including designing a course, assessing training needs, evaluation of training and appraisal.

6. Kettle, Melvyn (1986) *Employer's Guide to Disabilities* Woodhead-Faulkner

This book lists all the major disabilities, showing the range of difficulties which may be encountered, together with the points an employer would need to think about.

7. Connor, Helen, Strebler, Marie and Hirsh, Wendy (1990) *You and Your Graduates: The First Few Years* Institute of Manpower Studies Report No 191

8. Arnold, John (1986) Getting started: how graduates adjust to employment *Personnel Review* 15 1 : 16–20

The book (7) is a useful guide as it gives case studies taken from major UK organisations. It covers recruitment, induction, career management, training, performance review and feedback. The article (8) shows the kind of changes which graduates undergo in entering the workplace.

9. Megranahan, Michael (1989) *Counselling: A Practical Guide for Employers* Institute of Personnel Management

Everything you need to know about counselling your employees – how to improve your own counselling skills and when to call for outside help.

10. Stemp, Peter (1988) *Are You Managing?* Industrial Society

11. Morris, Michael (1988) *The First Time Manager* Kogan Page

Number 10 provides an overview of what a good manager needs to do, whereas number 11 is far more detailed. The latter covers not only what you need to do as a manager, but also has a chapter on each of the major functional areas, eg finance and marketing, and looks at the principles of management.

The last two books are recommended for reading from the personal, rather than the organisational, perspective. The first is a comprehensive and informative book on what individuals need to do to help themselves fit in with the organisation. The second is an annual publication, covering career planning. It contains exercises to help the reader decide on a career path. (It also looks at job hunting, but the American approach is rather different from that typically taken in the UK.)

12. Josefowitz, Natasha and Gadon, Herman (1988) *Fitting In: How to Get a Good Start in Your New Job* Addison-Wesley Publishing Company Inc., USA
13. Bolles, Richard Nelson (1991) *The 1991 What Color is Your Parachute?* Ten Speed Press, USA

Further information

Telephone advice and free information booklets are available from the Advisory, Conciliation and Arbitration Service (ACAS). The booklets cover induction of new employees, employee appraisal, absence, recruitment and selection, labour turnover, workplace communications, the company handbook, employment policies and discipline at work. There is also a handbook for small employers on employing people.

ACAS Head Office is at 27 Wilton Street, London SW1X 7AZ; 071-210 3000. They also have various regional offices (see your local telephone book).

Further information about disabilities can be sought from RADAR (The Royal Association for Disability and Rehabilitation) at 25 Mortimer Street, London W1N 8AB; 071-637 5400 or from Disablement Resettlement Officers who can be contacted through your local Jobcentre.

Professional bodies may also be able to give advice on aspects of induction specific to their industries.

Kogan Page publishes many titles of interest to personnel and training managers. A complete list is available on application to 120 Pentonville Road, London N1 9JN; 071-278 0433.

Index

Absenteeism 16, 123, 142, 144
Accident rates 76, 142, 144
Administrative arrangements 33, 49, 50, 54
Appraisals 24, 35, 36, 77, 118–19, 123, 145
Authority levels/limits 52, 58, 106

Belonging 17, 18, 24–5, 100
Briefing colleagues 32–3
Buddies 35, 53, 56–7, 142, 145, 146
Building the relationship 17, 51–3, 122

Career planning 125–6
Case studies 81
Company values 25, 31
Conformity 17, 27
Contracts
- behavioural 10, 20–27, 56, 78, 108
- formal 14, 20, 29–30, 50
- implied terms 30

Culture
- company 12, 14, 20–22, 79, 101, 110
- shock 109–10

Disabilities, people with 79, 83, 98–9
Discussion groups 81
Dismissal 15, 29, 35, 110, 124
Distant workers 100–101

Early leaving
- common causes of 14–16
- cost of 12–13

Employees' log books 88, 145
Ethnic minorities 52, 79, 102
Executives 106–8
Exit interviews 88, 142, 147
Expatriates 17, 108–10

False expectations 13, 14, 104–5
Fault rates 15, 16, 117, 123, 144
Feedback 49, 56, 84–5, 99, 105, 107, 113, 115, 116–20, 122, 124, 146, 148
Films and videos 80–81, 84
First impressions 9, 11, 14, 20, 23, 28

Goals and goal setting 84, 105, 120
Graduates 79, 80, 104–6, 115
Group dynamics 24, 25, 48, 108
Guest speakers 74, 77, 81

Health and safety 16, 18, 30, 51, 58, 76, 99, 103

Induction
- budget 10, 35, 36, 142
- costs 18, 73
- crisis 12
- definition 16
- evaluation 35, 142–9, 148
- manual 88
- objectives 9, 14
- period, length of 18, 72
- policy 35–6
- recipients 17, 72, 73

Induction course
- content 17, 75–7, 80
- design 10, 35, 72, 74–5, 87, 148
- evaluation 10, 13, 35, 84, 142, 147–8
- location 83
- piloting 83–4

Industrial groups 113–14
Information
- basic needs 48–51, 58, 75, 88
- company literature 14, 21, 22, 24, 31, 50–51, 76, 82–3
- further needs 121–2
- overload 17, 73, 85–6
- pre-employment 28–30
- rumours 33, 55, 83, 110

Instructions

first day 30–31
giving 26, 120–21
joining 17
Interviews, impact of 23
Introductions 31, 54–5, 56, 77, 106

Job description 14, 20, 29, 36, 52
Job satisfaction 16, 24
Jobsharers *see* part-time workers

Labour turnover 9, 12, 13, 73, 75, 76, 88, 142, 143–4
Learning
curves 18, 85, 116, 122, 145
self-managed 80, 104, 111
styles 10, 77–9, 80
theory 10, 77–9, 84–8
transfer of 84

Managers, as inductees 106–8
Meeting the team 11, 54–5, 57, 74
Memory and recall 77, 87–8
Mentors 57, 104, 106, 110, 115, 126, 142, 145, 146
Merit pay schemes 119–20
Motivation 10, 20, 26, 82, 83, 84–5, 87, 119

Non-verbal behaviour 23, 24

Offer letter 28–30
Older workers 112
Organisation charts 31, 52, 58, 82
Overhead projector slides 81, 83
Overselling the job 13, 14, 15, 84

Part-time workers 79, 99–100
Pay 12, 13, 14, 15, 17, 26, 119–20, 145
see also merit pay schemes
Peer pressure 22, 24–5, 108
Personality clash 15
Personnel, role of 34–5, 75, 142, 147, 148
Practical jokes 24–5
Presenteeism 20, 25, 111, 123, 144
Probationary period 15, 16, 35, 36, 52, 99, 110, 122–5
Productivity 10, 11, 13, 15, 16, 20, 106
Professionals 100–101
Progress checks 52, 54, 57–8, 100, 123
Project teams 110–11
Promotees 12, 16, 17, 32, 110–11, 124
Promotion 14, 15, 26, 84, 125

Qualitative measures 145–8
Quantitative measures 142–5
Questionnaires 78, 80, 82, 142, 143, 145–7

Redundancy, after 111–12
Role models 21, 77, 116
Rumours *see* information

School leavers 79, 102–4
Settling in 11, 16, 59, 74, 115–16
Shiftworkers 99–100
Sickness 123, 142, 144
Simulations 82
Skill development 85
Staff retention/turnover *see* labour turnover
Standard of work 11, 15, 16, 52–3, 76, 120, 122, 123, 124, 145
Stress 11, 52, 109, 123, 144
Surveys 142, 145–7

Tape/slide packs 81
Teambuilding 106–8
Temporary staff 17, 112–13
Terms and conditions 20, 28–9, 50–51, 73, 76, 77, 109
Trade union involvement 31, 55, 74, 77
Training
aids 80–83
budget 112
computer based 82
initial needs 13, 33–4, 56
methods 79–80, 85–7
Transferees 17, 110–11

Waste rates *see* fault rates
Welcome pack 22, 31–2, 52
Women returners 52, 79, 101–2